Working FROM THE Margins

Working FROM THE Margins

VOICES OF MOTHERS IN POVERTY

Virginia E. Schein

ILR PRESS AN IMPRINT OF
Cornell University Press
ITHACA AND LONDON

23.00

First published 1995 by ILR Press.
Second printing 1996 by ILR Press/Cornell University Press.

Library of Congress Cataloging-in-Publication Data
Schein, Virginia E.
    Working from the margins : voices of mothers in poverty / by
  Virginia E. Schein.
    p. cm.
  Includes bibliographical references (p.) and index.
  ISBN 0-87546-341-X (cloth : alk. paper).—
ISBN 0-87546-342-8 (pbk. : alk. paper)
    1. Poor women—United States—Case studies. 2. Women heads of households—United States—Case studies. 3. Single mothers—United States—Case studies. 4. Welfare recipients—United States—Case studies. I. Title.
  HV1445.S34   1995
  362.83'0973—dc20   94-47573

Printed in the United States of America

Cornell University Press strives to utilize environmentally responsible suppliers and materials to the fullest extent possible in the publishing of its books. Such materials include vegetable-based, low-VOC inks and acid-free papers that are also either recycled, totally chlorine-free, or partly composed of nonwood fibers.

Cloth printing   10 9 8 7 6 5 4 3 2 1

Paperback printing   10 9 8 7 6 5 4 3

To Alex and Rupert

Contents

Acknowledgments

I want to thank the women who shared their stories with me. Their words and experiences are the heart of this book.

Initial ideas for the research project came from my participation on the Job Training and Partnership Act's (JTPA) Private Industry Council (PIC) of Franklin and Adams counties and the board of directors of Survivors, Inc., a battered women's shelter. I want to thank the single mothers I met through these experiences and the council and board members, especially Richard Bonini, for providing me with useful background information.

I am indebted to Gettysburg College for granting me the sabbatical that allowed me to leave duties and campus to conduct my research and to the county assistance agencies who cooperated in the project. I also want to thank Amy Sozio and Jennifer Williams for their research assistance and Judy Hull for her assistance and support.

My thanks and gratitude are extended to Judy Hepler for typing each transcript with care (and speed), assisting me with the manuscript preparation, and enthusiastically supporting all aspects of this project.

I want to thank Jill Schumann for her many contributions to the perspective of this book.

My trust in Fran Benson, director of ILR Press, and her staff gave me the courage to move the manuscript from my desk into the world. I want to thank Fran, as well as Andrea Clardy, Patty Peltekos, and Faith Short for a rewarding and productive publishing experience.

My thanks to my son, Alex, for the laughter and inspiration that kept things in balance. The support of my husband, Rupert Chisholm, has been invaluable. I want to thank him for his encouragement, patience, and understanding throughout this project. The book is dedicated, with love and appreciation, to my son and my husband.

Working FROM THE Margins

ONE. **Think Single Mother, Think Poverty**

A mother with a small child in tow finishes her grocery shopping and starts to put her items on the checkout counter. Her daughter takes a pack of gum from the nearby stand and places it on the counter. The mother returns it quickly and pats the girl's head. It is not the cavities or excess sugar that worry her. She cannot afford the gum. To buy it would mean putting a milk or juice container back on the shelf.

A third-grade girl rushes into the house. She excitedly waves a school notice saying she can order a book and even subscribe to her own magazine. But after talking with her mother, she races out again, shouting, "I'm tired of being poor." The mother does not have the five dollars the school requires for the orders.

It is a warm July evening. Through the windows, a mother and her two children listen to the sounds of a carnival in town. They walk up the street. Standing on a small hill, they watch the Ferris wheel go around and spot the glow from the new rocket ride. The mother and the children walk slowly back home. The children look over their shoulders at the lights from the rides. Their mother does not have the money for the entrance fees.

These brief illustrations capture the day-to-day lives of mothers raising children in poverty. They are simple experiences, not the traumatic or fearful ones that also accompany lives in poverty. In their simplicity, they translate the meaning of poverty into everyday events. Similar economic hardships are incurred daily by approximately four million mothers and the eight million children in their families.

In 1978 Diana Pearce was among the first to document the rising percentage of poor families headed by women, which she termed the "feminization of poverty." Numerous studies continue to point out the impoverished status of the single mother (for example, Women and Poverty 1984; Garfinkel and McLanahan 1986; Pearce 1989; Harris 1993; Polakow 1993). Both the poverty rate and the number of poor families headed by women increased in 1991, and this change accounted for 64 percent of the net increase in poor families in 1990–91 (U.S. Bureau of the Census 1992). Currently, 45.7 percent of all female-headed families with children under eighteen are poor. By contrast, 17.7 percent of all families with children are poor. Of all poor families with children, 60 percent are female-headed households (U.S. Bureau of the Census 1993). No matter how you examine the statistics, they say the same thing. To think single mother is to think poverty.

For almost twenty years the economic difficulties of single mothers have not improved. Women parenting in poverty is still a significant concern. Does the impoverished condition of so many single mothers reflect an intractable problem that, despite our best efforts, can never be solved? Or is it possible that the right questions are not part of the public debate, and therefore most of our efforts are focused on addressing questions that have little to do with solving the problem?

Questioning the Question

The clue to understanding what direction our questions take is in the following: Most poor single mothers and their children are on welfare. Of all poor people in female-headed families, 85.5 percent are in households receiving some form of means-tested public assistance, other than school lunches (U.S. Bureau of the Census 1993). As such, society's focus, including that of the media and the government, tends to be on welfare and welfare reform, a focus that directs the kinds of questions asked. These questions include: How can we get the poor women off welfare and into jobs? How can we reform the welfare system so as to decrease the number of people it serves? How can we reduce the costs of welfare?

U.S. citizens *do* need answers to these questions. It would be fiscally irresponsible for the government to be unconcerned with the costs of its programs. But underlying these questions is the view that the welfare system is the problem. If we apply the appropriate reforms—some geared to getting the women off welfare and into jobs and others aimed at various forms of social engineering, often through punitive reforms—the problem will be solved. But what problem will be solved? At best, government payments to impoverished people will decrease. There may be fewer people on the welfare rolls, or those on welfare may receive less in assistance. As such, the cost of the welfare system will be lowered. The danger, or perhaps the reality, is that focusing on the welfare system can perpetuate the belief that these efforts are aimed at reducing poverty. It suggests that changing the system and decreasing the welfare rolls will address the problem of poverty among single mothers.

But this is a very narrow perspective. It focuses on one element, the welfare system, and equates reforming the system and moving women off the welfare rolls with solving the poverty issue. But does it? Nicholas Zill, Kristin Moore, Christine Nord, and Thumar Stief (1991) found that even substantial labor force participation does not necessarily bring single mothers out of poverty, primarily because of the low wages they earn. A 1991 U.S. General Accounting Office Report found that single mothers are vulnerable to layoffs, are lacking important fringe benefits, such as paid sick leave, and have high expenses for child care. They conclude that many single mothers will remain near or below the poverty line even if they have full-time jobs.

By keeping the welfare system and poverty so intertwined, we are asking questions that have little to do with reducing poverty among poor single mothers. Tinkering with the welfare system can lower some costs and reduce welfare rolls, but it may or may not reduce poverty. The rising number of single mothers who are living at or below the poverty level strongly suggests that we are asking the wrong questions and trying to solve the wrong problem.

The Narrow Perspective

Examining some of the attitudes and assumptions underlying the narrow perspective sheds further light on its limitations. Attempts to reduce welfare costs have prompted a trend toward punishing welfare recipients. In New Jersey, for example, welfare mothers who bear additional children are denied benefits for those children.

Punitive measures play into the myths, such as having babies for the money, about women on welfare. The myths justify the measures and the measures reinforce the myths. In New Jersey, before the restricted benefits law was enacted, a woman on welfare who had another child received an additional sixty-four dollars a month for that child. Given this increment, compared to the costs, time, and effort of raising a child, no one conducting cost-benefit analyses would ever conclude that having a baby was a way to make money.

Negative stereotypes about women with children on welfare seem to underlie the punitive approaches to reforming the system. Welfare is not a neutral term. "Welfare mother" usually connotes a lazy woman who doesn't want to work and who has children to avoid working. Welfare queen is a term that implies that welfare is a scam to avoid working. According to Angela Williams (1994), the contemporary image of the welfare mother is a lazy, even immoral woman, unwilling to work, with no aspirations beyond maximizing her take at the public trough.

The myth of the lazy and unmotivated welfare mother persists, despite many studies to the contrary (see Schiller 1973; Garvin, Smith, and Reid 1978; Davidson and Gaitz 1974; Marshall 1982; and Tienda and Stier 1991, among others). Two recent studies have found that the gain of additional welfare benefits is not related to having more children (Robins and Fronstin 1993; Rank 1994). Russell Hanson and John Hartman, in their 1994 study, found that poor mothers do not move from state to state in order to receive greater welfare benefits. Nonetheless, negative images about mothers on welfare continue to drive many public policies and proposals for welfare reform.

What purpose does negative stereotyping serve? As with any form of stereotyping, generalizing about the qualities of a group of people keeps us from seeing the group members as individuals, with differing characteristics, attributes, and experiences. In the case of mothers on welfare, it allows us to remain distanced from their plight. We don't have to see the mother on welfare as struggling, destitute, or in personal pain. That image can capture our attention. That voice says, "I need help." Rather, the generalized view of the lazy welfare mother allows us to close our eyes to her concerns and can even foster a blame-the-victim attitude. She is responsible for her situation.

Also underlying the punitive approaches are attempts at social engineering and the regulation of women's lives. Some measures seek to keep women in the traditional role of wife, others in low-paying "women's" jobs. Both, as argued by Mimi Abramovitz (1988) and Dorothy Miller (1990), among others, are solutions emanating from a patriarchal society that seeks to perpetuate women's dependence on men or male-dominated systems.

The narrow perspective uses cost reduction as a primary indicator of policy or program success. For example, evaluations of welfare-to-work programs look more at reductions in welfare payments and expenditures to the state than the significance of any earnings increases to the participants. Judith Gueron and Edward Pauly (1991), in their review of one set of welfare-to-work studies, state, "While . . . welfare-to-work programs modestly improved people's income, they proved unlikely to move people out of poverty. If reducing poverty is the goal, other types of policies . . . will be important complements" (p. 33). Indeed, a closer look at many successful welfare-to-work studies reveals that actual benefits to the participants are minimal. In one highly praised study, those in the welfare-to-work experiment earned more than the control group and received less in welfare payments (DeParle 1992). The increased earnings, however, were $2,500 per year as opposed to $1,500 per year. Each group still received welfare payments and few, if any, moved out of poverty.

Not all proposals to alter the welfare system are punitive or driven solely by cost containment. There is increasing acknowledgment of the need for basic support services for welfare-to-work programs, such as transportation and child care. Many of these components were included in the reforms of the late 1980s. The 1988 Family Support Act supports welfare-to-work programs through the Job Opportunities and Basic Skills (JOBS) Training Program. JOBS provides support services as well as training, education, and employment search opportunities. One recent study (Greenberg 1992) estimates that 10 percent of welfare parents throughout the nation are participating in JOBS programs.

Legislators currently deliberating welfare reform continue to focus on getting the recipients off welfare. They walk a tightrope, trying to balance punitive and supportive measures. Proposals that call for two-year limits on welfare speak to and reinforce the myth of the lazy, unmotivated welfare mother. But those that include training, education, child care, and other supports recognize some of the realities of the women's lives.

Yet, punitive or otherwise, the narrow perspective keeps us on the same merry-go-round of blaming the welfare system and the people in it for the continued rise in welfare costs and the number of welfare recipients. It does not address the causes of poverty or the impoverished circumstances of single mothers. There is nothing wrong with improving a system or reducing its costs. But focusing on changing the welfare system as a way to ameliorate the problem of poverty does not make any sense.

If we had an outbreak of a sickness and people flocked to the hospital for help, would we focus on ways to keep them out of the hospital in order to solve the sickness problem? Would we call those who went to the hospital "hospital dependent"? Would we reduce their hospital benefits so that they wouldn't want to come back to the hospital? Of course not. Rather, we would look at environmental factors, institutional factors, family factors, and individual factors to determine the cause of the sickness. We would do this by going directly to the sick people and examining their situations and the multiple factors that could be contributing to the disease.

This is the approach we need to take in order to reduce the poverty of women raising children alone. If we continue to follow the narrow perspective, the poor mothers and their children go nowhere. They remain in poverty. We need to reframe our questions, placing them within a much broader context. As Richard Caputo (1989) states, "Although proposed reforms link welfare with work, their aim is to reduce the welfare rolls, not poverty. A more appropriate goal would be to assist both the working poor and the hard to employ to escape poverty. It is as important to elevate and shift public debate from welfare reform to poverty reduction as it is to advocate for specific reform measures" (p. 95). Questions emanating from a broad viewpoint can direct us to solutions that address the problem of reducing poverty among single mothers.

A Broad Perspective

To address seriously the issue of single mothers and their families living in poverty, we need to take a broad perspective and pose a different set of questions. Who are the poor single mothers? What circumstances bring them to poverty? How do they live and raise their children? What is needed to help poor single mothers move out of poverty and into lives with opportunities for themselves and their children?

A broad perspective on the problem allows us to examine the multiple factors contributing to women's poverty and to recognize that changes on all fronts, including the welfare system, are necessary if we are to make progress in the long run. We can view the woman within the context of today's society and bring into focus factors limiting her economic progress, rather than attributing her circumstances solely to her own deficiencies. Within a broad perspective, a mother's application for welfare is viewed as a call for help. This is a compassionate perspective, one that recognizes the micro factors, such as family circumstances, and macro factors, such as gender discrimination in the workforce, that contribute to her situation.

At the macro level, a broad perspective is taken by those who look at the interplay between workplace discrimination and women's poverty. Wage differentials between men and women, occupational segregation, and discrimination in entry and advancement operate to keep women, more than men, in low-paying jobs. Women's wages are so low that women's full-time employment provides no automatic solution to female poverty (Corcoran, Duncan, and Hill 1984; Spalter-Roth, Hartmann, and Andrews 1990).

Addressing the issues of discrimination and wage differentials is one example of tackling women's poverty directly. Both the problems and the solutions have nothing to do with the welfare system.

But resolving such problems is difficult and might challenge many existing economic systems (see Smith 1984). How much easier it is for policy makers to blame the woman, view her as lazy, and rally around the cry of "get her a job." The narrow perspective, by blaming welfare and the women on it, keeps many poor single mothers going around in a revolving door. For example, LaDonna Pavetti (1993) found that of those who leave welfare for employment, 40 percent return within one year and 66 percent within five years. They do not progress out of poverty. Our focus on welfare and welfare reform prevents us from addressing the underlying social and economic issues that produce this revolving door.

If we followed a broad perspective, we would eliminate tinkering and blaming. Questions emanating from a broad perspective suggest solutions that encompass myriad approaches to resolving poverty among single mothers. For example, Pearce (1989, 1993) proposes looking at the needs of poor women and their families within the context of employment, occupational segregation, sexual harassment, child care, health care, antidiscrimination laws, housing, and the interactions of race, ethnicity, and gender as they affect poverty.

Proponents of the narrow perspective ask: How do we move poor women off welfare? The broad perspective considers: How do we improve the quality of life of poor women and their children and help them leave poverty permanently? If we are going to tackle successfully the problem of women parenting in poverty, we need to widen our focus on the issue.

Compassion in Context

What is needed to realign our thinking? How do we begin to see a woman's request for welfare assistance as a call for help? How do we transform the public debate so as to focus on questions that address the problem of poverty? To start with, we need to learn more about the women and to understand their current circumstances within the context of their lives. Such understanding can be the first step toward developing approaches that help poor mothers move out of poverty permanently.

The research upon which this book is based is designed as a study of compassion in context. I look at issues pertaining to poor single mothers and work within the context of their history and social circumstances. This approach moves away from denouncing a person for her circumstances and toward an understanding of such circumstances (Riger 1992). As discussed by Arnold Kahn and Janice Yoder (1989), many Americans believe that outcomes are due to choices made by free and self-determining individuals, implying that people get what they deserve. The contextual approach puts outcomes in perspective and brings to the forefront the various factors—individual, historical, and societal—that impinge on a situation. With such understanding we can begin to address the issues pertaining to the impoverished single mother.

This research focuses on the individual, and explores in-depth the lives of thirty poor single mothers, developing a rich and comprehensive picture of their lives. A secondary purpose is to present this picture to the reader through the women's voices. A research format that illustrates the experiences of the women so directly may help move the public debate toward the broad approach more readily than myriad statistics and proposals for change.

The Research Questions: Work in Context

A cursory look at the situation of impoverished single mothers suggests that the barriers to solid economic independence are enormous. These women usually possess limited educational and life skills (Cooper 1993). In the workplace they encounter discrimination in pay and job opportunities, sometimes accompanied by negative attitudes and devaluations of their abilities (Amott 1993; Amott and Matthaei 1991). As parents they struggle with the strains of work and family responsibilities, and as single parents they must cope with these multiple pressures alone (Morrison et al. 1986). Finally, financial concerns are a daily fact of life (Sidel 1986).

Furthermore, while each barrier alone is problematic, their occurrence in concert increases the complexity. What is the interaction between low-paying jobs and work-family conflicts? How does it all play out within the context of years of poverty, no family support, or poor health? One of the purposes of my research is to gain an understanding of the full range of these barriers and their interactions within the life circumstances of the women. I look at not only work issues but also early life experiences, relationships, financial concerns, and child raising. With such information, we can design and implement approaches that can effectively facilitate the women's exit from poverty and their entrance into lives of dignity and opportunity.

Members of various disciplines have studied poor women and work as a societal issue. Analyses of demographics and labor force participation, studies of welfare families over time (such as the Panel Study of Income Dynamics), and program and training evaluation efforts contribute valuable information to the issue (for example, Corcoran et al. 1984; Garfinkel and McLanahan 1986; Ellwood 1988; Harlan and Steinberg 1989; Bane and Ellwood 1994). It is the individual level of study, however, that can introduce the differing attitudes and experiences of the women as they move toward economic independence.

In the late 1960s and early 1970s, applied psychological research focused on the work experiences of the poor. Most of these efforts looked at job training as a means of facilitating a cultural transition from being unemployed to being employed full-time. The poor were referred to as the hard-core unemployed (HCU), and most of the HCUs studied were males (for example, Friedlander and Greenberg 1971). Virginia O'Leary (1972) studied seventy-two black females in an experimental investigation that, in her words, "boomeranged." Some women participated in role-playing and group problem-solving training sessions as a way to improve their job experiences, others did not. The levels of self-esteem and positive feelings of the women in the experimental group were raised. Contrary to expectations, however, these women were also more likely to leave the job. The jobs were highly structured and repetitious, the pay was low, and the opportunities for advancement were not immediate. With elevated self-esteem, the women were more likely to try to move on to more suitable and rewarding job situations. O'Leary concludes,

"Training aimed at re-socialization without consideration of the nature of the job . . . may be ineffective if not detrimental" (p. 494).

Leonard Goodwin (1972), in a questionnaire study of work orientations, found that both women on welfare and women not on welfare placed the same high value on the work ethic. Welfare women, however, were more insecure about their ability to achieve job success. He observes, "If jobs are ill-paid and regarded as 'make work,' they may prove even more discouraging to the poor than no jobs at all. Welfare recipients . . . should not be denied opportunity, but the training and support should be of the quality that makes occupational success a reasonable probability" (p. 115).

Studies such as Goodwin's point out the complex issues underlying the problem of poor women and work, problems that go well beyond a simplistic "get a job" solution. These studies raise enticing questions, such as: What happened to those women with raised hopes who left the repetitious jobs? If women on welfare are motivated to work, then what are the factors that impede their entrance into or advancement in the workplace? Unfortunately, the applied psychological research on the poor and work was cut short before it could produce more information about impoverished single mothers. As society's interest in the "war on poverty" declined, so too did this type of research on the work experiences of the poor.

Since the late 1970s, the field of industrial and organizational psychology, which focuses on the individual in the workplace, has ignored poor women altogether. A review of articles published in the *Journal of Applied Psychology*, the field's premier publication, from 1978 to the present revealed no research on poor women's work experiences. Furthermore, the field of psychology in general provides little help in understanding the broader issues of poor women. Pamela Reid (1993) decries the limited attention paid to poor women within psychology. Searching a psychological research database for the years 1984–91, she found that only slightly more than half of 1 percent of all the research abstracts that contained the word "woman" also contained "poverty," "working class," or "low income." She describes poor women in psychological research as "shut up and shut out."

At the individual level, the issues of poor women and work need more research attention. Moreover, we need to explore these issues within the context of the women's past and present circumstances. Doing so can provide us with a realistic awareness of their situations and can enrich efforts within the broad perspective. Two studies illustrate the value of including the context of life circumstances. John Weidman, Richard White, and B. Katherine Swartz

(1988) described a training-program evaluation study in which only 29 percent of all the women who enrolled in a male-dominated electronic technician training program graduated. A wide variety of factors circumscribed their efforts to succeed. These included child-care arrangements; transportation problems; personal finances; health problems; racial, sexual, and antiwelfare prejudicial remarks from the faculty and other students; negative reactions from children; criticisms from family members; and incidents of violence from boyfriends and husbands who were opposed to this training. This study points up the multitude of factors that can constrain a woman as she seeks to gain economic independence and highlights the importance of understanding work within the context of life circumstances.

Deborah Belle's 1982 study, *Lives in Stress*, provides a comprehensive look at the life circumstances of poor women. Belle and her colleagues studied the lives of forty-three poor women and their families in depth. During the project they visited the homes and interviewed the children, as well as the women. Although their focus was on mental health and depression, they examined the full range of life areas, including work, the welfare system, discrimination, social support, parenting, children, poverty, and early life history. They concluded, "Seen in the context of human lives, depression appears an almost unavoidable response to an environment that allows women little control over most of the important things in life and little hope that life will improve. The long-term problems of poverty, burdensome responsibilities, and foreclosed opportunity contribute more heavily to the depression of low-income mothers than a single crisis or traumatic event" (p. 241).

Understanding of poor women and work begins with a full consideration of their lives. Much can be learned from looking in depth at the women within the context of their circumstances.

The Research Approach: Tell Me Your Story

One purpose of compassion in context is to bring the realities of the women's lives as close to the reader as possible. The research outcomes are presented here through the voices of the impoverished mothers. Although the analysis focuses on category development, the voices used to determine and define these groupings are presented to the reader in full. Pamela Reid (1993) observes that "the silencing of poor women in psychological research has resulted from reliance on expert testimony, that is, a reliance on our own interpretations of the experience of others. We have not provided sufficient mechanisms to allow diverse groups of women to tell their own stories" (p. 144).

The interview approach was the main method of gathering data. Some scholars criticize qualitative methods, such as interviewing, as too subjective and open-ended, and arguments are made for the objectivity of traditional approaches. But the objectivity required of quantitative approaches, such as experimental studies or quantitative hypothesis testing methods, may contribute to our lack of understanding of or compassion for those in impoverished circumstances. Quantitative techniques require and thus encourage a distancing from the people under study. It is possible to draw assumptions and make generalizations without direct experiential knowledge of the people in the research (see arguments of Mulvey 1988; and Gardner, Dean, and McKaig 1989, among others).

Qualitative approaches, on the other hand, provide an opportunity, albeit briefly, to see the world from another person's point of view. Such experiential knowledge is essential if we are to address problems from the perspective of those in need. Indeed, qualitative proponents argue that greater closeness, rather than greater distance, underlies meaningful inquiry. According to sociologist Herbert Blumer (1970), "The task of scientific study is to lift the veils that cover the area of group life that one proposes to study. The veils are not lifted by substituting . . . preformed images for firsthand knowledge. The veils are lifted by getting close to the area and digging deep into it through careful study" (pp. 31–32). In a similar vein, ethnographer John Irwin (1987) states, "Human behavior and social existence is a subjective and willful construction and requires drawing close to subjects in their natural contexts and understanding the fundamental human process" (p. 41).

The voices of poor women are often buried in statistical reports analyzing the success or failure of a program, or they are lost in stereotypes portraying welfare women as passive, disinterested in work, or unable to hold jobs. Stereotypes and statistics can be ignored, real people cannot. If we can peel away the negative connotations of "welfare mother" and listen to the voices of impoverished single mothers, we can obtain a thorough understanding of their needs and the realities of their circumstances.

The Research Women: Beyond the Stereotype

Another purpose of the research was to bring to the forefront the voices of women who don't fit the stereotype of the welfare mother: women in small towns and rural areas. According to Kathryn Porter (1989), most Americans perceive poverty as predominantly an urban issue. The inner-city welfare mother has come to represent the poor in the minds of much of the general public and policy makers. In *Poverty in Rural America*, Porter found that poverty rates are higher in rural than in metropolitan areas and that more than one out of four poor Americans live outside of a metropolitan area.

The rural poor are often overlooked, in both policies and research. Paul Dudenhefer (1993), using the *Social Sciences Index*, a major bibliography of published works in the social sciences, found that during an eleven-year period, only twenty-one articles were listed under "rural poor: U.S." This compares with twenty-six articles on the urban poor in 1991–92 alone. As he states, "When researchers . . . think poverty, they think city, not town and country." Both Porter and Dudenhefer also observe that rural tends to be viewed as synonymous with farm, although in 1990 only 8 percent of all rural inhabitants lived on farms (Dudenhefer 1993).

Although more impoverished single mothers live in metropolitan areas than in nonmetropolitan areas, the poverty rates do not vary by region. Porter found that in both metropolitan (cities and suburbs) and nonmetropolitan areas (small towns and rural areas), families headed by single women are far more likely to be poor than families headed by two parents and that the poverty rates are about the same in both areas. In 1987, the poverty rate for people living in families headed by women was almost identical for non-metropolitan areas (44.8 percent) and central cities (44.4 percent).

Most of our research efforts and our thinking focus on the urban poor. For example, John Weidman, Richard White, and B. Katherine Swartz's study was done in Chicago and Columbus, Virginia O'Leary's study in Detroit, and Deborah Belle's study in Boston. Leonard Goodwin's large samples came from urban sites or surrounding suburbs of these sites. Although more than 40 percent of female-headed families in small towns and rural areas are living in poverty, research on poor women and work that looks at women in small towns is limited. One purpose of this research is to begin to balance our efforts by looking at women in small towns and rural areas. Since studies are needed that incorporate the voices of a varied group of poor women, the research also includes women in urban areas.

By focusing more on small-town and rural women than on urban women, this study also takes a small step toward untangling race and poverty. Because the majority of nonmetropolitan (small-town and rural) poor are white, the group of women includes more white women than women of color. Poverty is often equated with race, and the image of the inner-city welfare mother is that of a nonwhite, usually black, mother. Yet Isaac Shapiro, in *White Poverty in America* (1992), presents a somewhat different picture of race and poverty. Of the 35.7 million poor people in 1991, about half, 17.7 million, are white. Although minorities are more likely to be poor, whites make up the single largest group of poor people, and by a large margin.

In female-headed families with children, the poverty rate among whites rose from 27.6 percent in 1979 to 31.5 percent in 1989, and in 1991 more than one out of every three white female-headed families with children (34.9 percent) lived in poverty. Although in 1991 a plurality of poor female-headed families (44.5 percent) were black, nearly two of every five poor female-headed families with children (37.5 percent) were white (Shapiro 1992).

If we are to address the issue of impoverished single mothers, we need to see the whole face of poverty and not focus on just one part. We need to expand our thinking about poor women to include those in small towns as well as inner cities. We also need to untangle race from images of poverty. A single white mother living in a small town is as much a part of the poverty picture as the single black inner-city mother.

When we look beyond the stereotypes, the women's attitudes and circumstances may be surprising and run counter to commonly held views. In addition, when we listen to the voices, the image can be of a white woman or a woman of color, of a small-town woman or an inner-city woman. But both the voice and the image will be of a mother raising her children, alone and impoverished.

TWO. **The Women**

I listened to thirty women talk about working and about their lives as single mothers. The stories they told reflected complexity, pain, and courage in trying to raise children in impoverished circumstances. Each woman was unique in the reasons for her difficulties and how she struggled to overcome them. But there was a commonality among their experiences, circumstances, and attitudes that allowed general themes to emerge. Looking at all the women was the only way to get the full picture of the life of the impoverished single mother. In gathering the stories, it was as if I held in my hand a translucent round gemstone with many different colored facets. If I turned it one way, one aspect was prominent. As I turned it another way, a different facet sparkled at me. And the more I turned it, the more I saw its depth and complexity. Each woman's story contributed to the development of the larger picture, with its common themes, that emerged from the research process.

Who Are the Women?

My initial contact with the women was made with the cooperation and assistance of five county assistance agencies in a large state in the eastern United States. Each office provided the names of women who were single heads of households, receiving some form of public assistance, raising one or more children eighteen years old or younger, and who have or had some form of work experience. Interviews were then arranged with each of the thirty women. Each interview, approximately sixty to ninety minutes long, covered basic demographics, work experiences, and past and present life experiences. The appendix details the sample selection, interview format, and procedures. All names used, including those of the women, the people to whom they refer, local or state programs, and areas, towns, and cities are pseudonyms.

Basic Demographics

The average age of the thirty women interviewed was 31.6, with a range of 21 to 42 years. Approximately half of the women had one or two children and half from three to five children. Eighteen of the women had been married and twelve had never married. The average age of the woman at the birth of her first child was 19.5, with a range of 15 to 28 years. Sixteen of the women graduated from high school and fourteen left school before graduation. Of the fourteen who dropped out of school, six have since obtained a general equivalency diploma (GED).

Twenty of the women live in small and medium-size towns and rural areas and ten live in metropolitan areas. Nine of the women are African-American or of mixed racial background and the remainder Caucasian, reflective of the nonurban areas in which well over 90 percent of the single mothers are Caucasian.

The Financial Situation

The average income for the women in the interview sample is $7,802 per year. The women vary in the extent to which they receive county assistance benefits. Sixteen of the women are not currently employed and receive full county assistance benefits, which include a cash grant, food stamps, and a medical card. Their average annual cash income is $4,955 per year.

Eleven of the women are employed less than full time. The average annual cash income of ten of them is $10,615; one woman did not report income. Six of these women also receive food stamps and some medical assistance, two women have medical benefits only, and one just receives food stamps. Two women are in transition from public assistance to work: they are newly engaged in part-time jobs and receive some cash as part of their annual incomes, as well as food stamps and medical benefits.

Two women are employed full-time and have just gone or are about to go off of public assistance completely. Their average annual income is (or will be) $15,162. One woman relies on child support payments of $10,504 and receives food stamps and medical benefits. Although child support payments are included in all of these annual income figures, its contribution, except for the one woman, is minimal. Only thirteen of the women receive some child support on a regular basis. Of these thirteen, eight are on full county assistance and therefore receive only fifty dollars per month of the support payments.

Employment Situation

The job titles of the eleven part-time workers are: file clerk, barber, waitress (two women), bartender, nurse's aide, occupational therapist's aide, dietary aide, telemarketing representative, hospital billing clerk, and food-processing plant employee. Of the two women employed full-time, one works as a paralegal and the other as a customer service representative. In addition to these thirteen women, three of the women recently completed post–high school education and training. Two of the women are graduates of a two-year college program and a third is a graduate of a two-year dental technician training program. All three are actively seeking full-time positions in their new fields.

The other fourteen women are in varying stages of moving from county assistance to employment as their primary source of income. One woman has definite job reentry plans as a waitress. Another plans to rely mainly on child support payments. Seven women are in math and grammar skills courses, which are early but first steps toward employment preparation. Of the remaining five, whose time on assistance ranges from six months to three years, their varied situations include medical problems, limited job opportunities, and unusual personal circumstances.

Julie: A Closer Look

Summarizing the overall characteristics of the group is one way to get an overview of the women. Another way is to take a closer look at the flow of events and circumstances in the life of one woman.

Julie, thirty-five, a white woman, is divorced and the mother of two elementary-school-age children. She lives in a medium-size town. She left her parents' home when she was eighteen but she had supported herself from the age of fifteen. Julie's early years included physical and sexual abuse by family members. She was raised to believe that women were of little value and had no rights.

Julie, a high school graduate, has worked mostly clerical jobs paying minimum wage or slightly higher. She quit working when she married at the age of twenty-six. She had two children and did not return to work until near the end of her marriage. Julie describes her husband as mentally abusive, with the potential for physical abuse. She left him three years ago. At that time, she was employed part-time in a supermarket. Unable to get evening child care, she was forced to quit her job shortly after leaving her husband. She then went on public assistance and has been on full benefits, including cash, food stamps, and medical coverage, for the last three years. She receives $396 a month from the state and the welfare office passes through $50 per month from her husband's $160 a month child-support payments. She and her two children live on $5,352 a year, significantly less than the 1993 U.S. poverty threshold of $11,642 for a family of three.

Julie enrolled in a job-training program two years ago. Initially fearful and full of doubt, she was encouraged and supported by the program counselors to take college classes. For the last two years she has been a full-time college student, commuting once or twice a day and raising her two young children. In addition to a tuition grant, she received transportation and child-care help from the program. Julie has just completed her degree in computer applications and graduated with a 3.72 average. She is actively seeking full-time employment.

Research Analyses and Framework Development

Both the overview of the group's characteristics and the closer look at one woman's flow of life circumstances capture aspects of who the women are. Because the major analyses focused on the determination of themes and categories reflective of the lives of the thirty women, the interview transcript data were analyzed for recurring topics. These topic areas were reviewed and examined, allowing for major categories and themes to emerge from the data. Subcategories were formed in a similar way. Eventually a framework of major and minor categories emerged.

The analysis process drew from the phenomenological approach of Robert Bogdan and Steven Taylor (1975) and borrowed from the thrust of Barney Glaser and Anselm Strauss's (1967) grounded-theory perspective. Although categories, not theories, were the outcomes, a primary focus was on remaining grounded in the words of the women.

The framework of major and minor categories forms the basis of chapters 3–8. Within each chapter, the women's voices shape and illustrate the outcome categories. The research outcomes, then, are the categories across and within the six core chapters. There were no substantive differences in the categories or themes that emerged between the rural and the urban women; therefore, the voices of all the women are blended appropriately into the category illustrations. One minor exception is the differing concerns with housing and transportation. In that section, found in chapter 8, the rural and urban voices are separated.

The Background Sketches

Because no one woman can represent the group, individual biographies, found at the end of the book, summarize the basic details of the lives of each of the thirty women. It may be helpful to refer to the background sketches to add contextual details to the women's voices, as each speaks to a circumstance or of an attitude reflecting a research theme.

The Environmental Context: Where Do They Live?

The thirty women live in a variety of settings. Eight women live in small towns, with populations ranging from 650 to 4,000. Eight live in medium-size towns, of from 7,000 to 17,000 people. Four women live in rural areas, five to ten miles from either a small or medium-size town. Ten of the women live in the central parts of cities; two in a small city, with a population of approximately 43,000; and eight in a very large metropolitan city, with a population of well over one million.

Some of the women live in small towns like Albertsville and Moss. Albertsville and the surrounding county is totally rural. Its location, nestled behind a small mountain range, gives it a very isolated quality, which is felt by its residents and visitors alike. On foggy days, which are common, and during the snowy winter months, people can't cross the mountain to get to work in a larger town.

Albertsville is small, with a crossroads at the center and more residences than stores on the main street. The town's rural nature is reflected in the large number of jeeps and trucks on its streets, as well as by the high proportion of vehicles equipped with gun racks and hunting rifles.

Moss, also very small, is less rural and isolated. Easily accessible from a main highway, it has one long main street with eight to ten cross streets. An elementary school is on one of the cross streets and nearby are small clapboard houses.

Several women live in medium-size towns, such as Telmont. The town has a center square and a large municipal building and several churches near the square. Fast-food restaurants and some discount stores are arrayed outside of the center. Further out are some light manufacturing facilities. Telmont is home to a private college and a branch of a community college.

Characteristic of most of these small and medium-size towns is their location within rural rather than urban areas. These are not towns adjacent to large metropolitan areas, but rather self-sufficient communities well removed from urban centers. Farms can be found within a mile or two of many of the small and medium-size towns.

Some women also live in rural areas some distance from even the smallest of towns. Reaching these rural locations usually means driving on dirt roads, unmarked except for a landmark, such as a barn. The children in rural areas and very small towns are bused to a high school serving numerous small areas.

By contrast, a few women live in the small city of Bridgeton. It is a densely populated city, and its housing is primarily row houses and two- or three-story renovated houses. Parts of Bridgeton, an old industrial city, are slowly being renovated; however, sections of the central city are still quite rundown. Bridgeton is ringed by shopping malls and several large factory/industrial complexes.

Finally, several of the women live in the large city of Dunmore. With a population of 1.5 million, it is a cosmopolitan city, with the expected array of entertainment, educational, and shopping facilities. Housing is a mix of high-rise buildings, row houses, and town houses converted into apartments. While parts of Dunmore are serene and elegant, other parts are severely rundown and crime-ridden. Almost all of the women who lived in this city referred to the drugs and guns in their neighborhoods. Dunmore has industrial and manufacturing sites near its outskirts, and service-sector and information technology employment centers throughout the city and environs.

The Women in Their Homes

Descriptions of the homes and environs of nine of the women provide a closer look at the women in these settings.

Rural Vistas

To reach one woman's home, I drove over a mountain range, then through one small town to an even smaller one. It consists of a post office, a church, an elementary school, and a convenience store. I turned at the town's crossroads, and drove another five miles, past a few houses and farms, separated from each other by at least a half mile.

The woman lived in a small house near the road. Her closest neighbor was some distance away. Her house, with a living room and small kitchen downstairs and three bedrooms upstairs, was bright and sunny inside, and the living room windows looked out on the countryside. On the wall were pictures of her five children. The furnishings were simple and neat, and family souvenirs and small decorative objects were on the tables.

Another rural woman lived about six miles from a medium-size town. Her trailer court, with about twelve trailers, was surrounded by open fields. Her trailer space was small, consisting of a tiny kitchenette, living room space, two bedrooms, and a bath. Laundry hung on a makeshift porch in front. As I sat in the living room waiting for her to put her child on the school bus for kindergarten, I noticed all the pictures on the tables and on the walls. There were several photos of her child. A framed certificate from a job training program held a prominent position on one wall, and another framed achievement certificate was on the table.

Small-Town Perspectives

On the outskirts of one small rural town, I drove down a dirt road, through a trailer park, to reach the home of another woman. Hers was a very large brick house, encircled by a porch, on which children's toys and bicycles were scattered. Two horses grazed across from the house. Next to the house was an abandoned garage or summer kitchen. The exterior of the house was quite rundown, with loose or falling bricks and shaky or broken porch posts and floorboards. The woman opened a side door and led me directly into a very large kitchen. All of the appliances were very old, but the room was neat and in order. There were several large rooms on the first floor, most of which were unfurnished. In the living room was an old rug and one chair. While the neatness reflected effort, the surroundings spoke of the absence of money to buy or even repair anything. We drank coffee and talked over her large, well-worn wooden kitchen table.

Another woman I visited lived on the ground level of a small, two-story white shingle house, on a side street lined with similarly small, well-kept houses and large trees. Cornfields were a few blocks away. Her home consisted of a living room, kitchen, bedroom, and bath. At the far end of the living room was a screen, behind which were her bed and chest. A small bathroom was off of the living room. The kitchen and her child's bedroom were in the back of the house. Sunlight streamed through the kitchen windows. The small rooms were immaculate and very cheery, and pictures decorated most of the walls. There was a dog on the small back porch. In the closet was a cat feeding her newborn kittens. Although the living spaces were small, their appearance spoke of a woman's efforts to make it a home for herself and her child.

In-Town Views

Several women lived two or three blocks from the center squares of medium-size towns. One rented half of what she described as an "old, big, ugly green house." Her street and those surrounding it have equally old and not-very-well-maintained houses. She and her children lived on the ground level, which had a kitchen, living room/dining room, and one and one-half bedrooms. I entered through the back door, which was close to the sidewalk, into the small kitchen. The dining area was cluttered with toys, children's games, and piled-up puzzles. The furniture was old and shabby. The woman disliked the house and the neighborhood and was hoping to be able to move her children to a larger place in a safer neighborhood.

Another woman lived with her five children in part of a large, old wooden house converted into four apartments. It was on a side street, across from a small group of stores. The front of her apartment faced the street and a narrow alley ran along one side. The first floor consisted of a very small kitchen and a living room. Upstairs were three small bedrooms and a bath, and a bedroom space on the attic level. Although the house was in need of external repairs, the interior furnishings were simple and neat. A large picture of the woman and her children was on the living room wall. It was summer and noise from the passing cars came through the open windows. As we talked, her two youngest children played in the alley close to the house.

Living at Home

A few women lived with family members or in family-owned residences. One woman lived with her infant daughter in the rear section of her mother's beauty shop. The shop, on a quiet street in a small town, was part of a duplex, similar to other duplexes on the street. I walked down the driveway to the back door. Her living room was tiny and seemed to be a converted back porch. Next to it was a kitchen, only slightly larger. Upstairs was a bedroom and a bath. The beauty shop took up the rest of the house. We sat and talked in the porch room, which overlooked the backyard. She held and played with her baby. On the floor was a large bassinet decorated by her mother. It was encircled by ten tiny handmade dolls.

I visited another woman who lived with her children in the basement of her parents' home, at the end of a dirt road. While at one time the area was probably not very populated, it was now surrounded by housing developments. Barefoot and smiling, she met me at the door and led me quickly down the narrow cellar stairs to the basement. It was converted into one large room, with a kitchenette arrangement at one end. At the other end were bunk beds for her children and a bed for her. Next to the kitchenette was a small table for eating, and a well-worn couch and chair were in the middle of the room. There was a shower in the basement room, but the bathroom was upstairs. The walls were gray cinder block and there were no windows. Several pictures of her children were on the table next to the chair. Except for the bathroom and the telephone, she and her children did not use the upstairs living areas.

City Life

One of the city participants lived in a low-income housing project in the small city of Bridgeton. The complex consisted of rows of two-story apartments, each with grassy plots in the front and back. Several winding streets run through the complex, which is off of a busy thoroughfare close to a few factories. The general area was poorly maintained. As I approached her door in the early morning, loud music could be heard from the apartment next door. The woman's home was quite small. Downstairs was a living room, kitchen, and bath, and there were two bedrooms upstairs. The walls were painted a light pink and the small couch and throw rug were coordinated with the wall coloring and other decorative features. A wreath was on the front door. In the back was a small flower garden. The rooms were warm, cheery, and upbeat. The woman was out when I arrived and her sister let me in. Later, she came rushing through the back door, her arms filled with fresh vegetables just purchased at the early morning farmer's market in the town center.

Enter the Women

With these environmental settings in mind, the stage is set for the voices of the women to reveal and illustrate various aspects of parenting in poverty.

THREE. The ABC's of Poverty and the Single Mother

Why are women raising children alone almost as likely to live in poverty as not? Why are these women in need of society's help in order to survive? Although all thirty stories are different, the same two, and in many cases three, factors seem to underlie the women's impoverished circumstances. I call them the ABC's of poverty and the single mother. "A" is the absence of the education and training necessary to qualify for a well-paying job; "B" is the betrayal by the mate, the father of the children; and "C" is negative childhood experiences and nonsupportive family influences. The first two, in combination, precipitate a woman's decline into poverty. The third factor, when present, contributes to the decline and undermines efforts to climb out of poverty.

Absence of Requisite Education and Job Skills

Almost all of the women lack the appropriate education and training necessary for jobs paying enough to support themselves and their families. It is not that the women did not work. Indeed, a frequent statement was "I have always worked." But it is the nature of the jobs that they are able to get that keeps them in poverty. The women are in jobs paying minimum wage or slightly higher. The jobs offer no advancement opportunities, reasonable benefits, job security, or flexibility. They pay little and go nowhere.

Sally: *"I started working when I was thirteen, at a restaurant washing dishes. It was mostly restaurant work when I was in school. After I got married I started in factories—shoe factories, clothing factories."*

LaVerne: *"I've baby-sat, worked in restaurants, on construction, in sewing factories, food factories, a dog-bone factory. Most of the jobs were minimum wage. At the sewing factory, it was piecework pay. If you sat there all day long except for your half-hour break, you'd make seven or eight dollars an hour."*

Anita: *"I waitress. I have always waitressed. I have been a waitress since I was sixteen."*

Carla: *"The first job I ever had was washing dishes. I was sixteen. In my next job I did telephone selling. I worked in a grocery store, being a cashier or whatever was needed. I cleaned offices."*

Jean: *"I was a bean cook."*

Vicki: *"I worked at Wendy's for quite a while. I was at Tompee factory before I got laid off. Then I was at Flick's, I got laid off there. Then I worked in a wood shop. I was there three years and then I went to the nursing home. There I was in housekeeping and a nurse's aide. All of these were full-time jobs. When I started at the nursing home I earned $5.25 per hour. When I left it was up to $7.75."*

Marie: *"When I was in high school I was a dishwasher. Even before that I cleaned school desks. I worked in a couple of fruit-packing companies. I was a waitress. You do what you have to do."*

Susan: *"I started out my first job ever as a dishwasher at a truck stop. Then I was a cook and a waitress, another job as a waitress, and finally a hostess."*

All of these jobs are low-paying, do not provide opportunities for earnings increases, and usually do not have adequate medical benefits programs. Moreover, these kinds of jobs offer very little job security. People in these jobs are easily replaced. A woman needing some flexibility due to child-related needs is more likely to be let go than given a break.

Julie: *"I went to work [at the supermarket] and told them I could not work nights anymore because of the two children. The manager had a ten o'clock meeting at night. It is one of the coldest winters in history. My oldest daughter has asthma. He said, 'You will be there at that meeting or you'll get fired.' I said, 'I can't bring my children out in that kind of weather.' Find a baby-sitter. I can't find a baby-sitter, not at ten at night. He said, 'Either you be at the meeting or you are fired.' So I quit."*

LaVerne: *"I was working at the dog-bone factory. My daughter had so many problems with her ears. She has had tubes in and out. Her tonsils and adenoids came out. She had gotten sick when I was working and I missed work and I kept missing work because of taking her to the doctors and getting her operations done, and I got fired."*

For Julie and LaVerne, the loss of a job pushed them onto public assistance. For most of the women, asking for such help wasn't a choice, it was a necessity.

Gloria: *"I had five children, my youngest was nine. I was working as a waitress for minimum wage. My daughter got sick, I couldn't afford to take her to the doctors. It was very rough. It was very frustrating not being able to buy groceries, not having enough food, trying to make meals out of nothing. Not being able to take them to the doctors was the most frustrating. When she really got sick, that's when I realized that I can't do this. It was hard on my pride but I did it. I didn't like to do it but I went on public assistance."*

Sixteen of the women graduated from high school and fourteen dropped out before graduation. While some of the women (seven) dropped out of high school to have a baby, an equal number of women (seven) simply quit school. Except for one woman, they were not encouraged by their families to stay in school. Some were needed in the workplace and others were raised to view marriage and motherhood as the most acceptable future for a woman.

Both Judy and Jessie left high school before graduation.

Judy: *"I went to the ninth grade. Then when I was sixteen I went to work. Mom and Dad was in debt so I helped them out with their bills."*

Jessie: *"At fourteen I was looking at marriage. In the 1950s you were more or less raised to be a housewife. Your husband supported you and you stayed home. Cook, clean, sew, wash, and iron, that's what I thought I was going to do. That's what I tried to do. But when he got laid off and I was needed to work, I didn't have any education and could not get a decent job so I did menial jobs. I was happy at the time. I didn't care. But now I need to make higher wages. Two of my kids are only in elementary school. I would really like to go to school and get some kind of education where I can make decent money. But I feel like I am getting too old. I'll be forty this year."*

Among those who graduated from high school, only one went on for further training, in an art school. But the high school graduates did not fare much better than those who dropped out of school. Although they had diplomas, they did not have any specific marketable skills. Lacking guidance and preparation for a particular vocation, they tended to hold the same types of jobs—in factories, as waitresses, as nurse's aides—as the school dropouts.

Many of the women were discouraged from advancing further in school, had no female models in jobs other than the low-level types, or were not guided by parents or teachers to think about their employment futures. Only one woman said her mother had a dream for her to go to college. Unfortunately, limited or thwarted ambitions and dead-end, low-paying jobs can lead to poverty when the woman is put into the position of family provider.

Betrayal by the Mate

The second common factor is betrayal by the man, the father of the children. The men varied in the nature of their betrayal to the women and the children. Some were abusive, were addicts, were poor providers relying on the women for financial support, or were simply disappearing dads. In the cases of abuse and addiction, leaving the man was the only hope for the mother and her children to have a chance at a more normal existence. Similarly, women whose men were jobless, had disappeared, or just dropped in and out were also put in the position of being the sole provider out of necessity.

These betrayals have two negative effects on the women. Not only are they thrust into the position of being sole family caretaker and provider, but they also have to deal with the effects of the betrayal on the children. Years of a father's absence, his alcoholic incidents, or his mistreatment of the children require explaining and healing efforts by the mother.

The Abusive Mate

Over one-third of the men fell into this category, with physical abuse being the primary form of mistreatment. Almost all of the women who described abusive relationships had been married to the men.

Amelia told her story while sitting in a small, sun-filled living room, with pictures of herself and her elementary-school-age son and daughter on the walls. Amelia was the only woman in the sample who had held a well-paying job. A high school graduate, she developed skills enabling her to supervise large numbers of people in an office in a large city. Initially she described her life as a single parent in a way not congruent with her poor surroundings. She had worked, earned a good salary, managed child care, and had a nice apartment. But her husband, she said, *"was an alcoholic. He was never there. When he was there we never knew if he would come crawling in the door or who was crawling in with him. The kids have seen their father out in the front yard just drink from morning to night. When I was married, he rarely worked. I finally left him.*

"I went to his house to collect child support. He and his friends had been drinking. I said, 'Look, I'm not here to cause any trouble. I just want my child support.' I held out my hand to get it and I got hit. That's the last thing I remember. When I came to I was in the emergency room. My son, then seven, went across the street to the neighbors and called 911. My face was destroyed. He had stepped on my face and I don't know to this day if he was the only one that did this. My nose and cheekbone have since been reconstructed. I was a mess. This is a heck of a lot of meanness out of one person.

"He did it in front of my kids and that's the one thing I will never forgive him for. He hit me before, but that was the last time. I left everything, went to a shelter, and then moved here. He does not know where I am. My children are still afraid. They sleep with the windows closed, even in the summer.

"I thought that once you were married you took your vows until death do you part. I didn't know he was supposed to kill you."

Gloria, a divorced mother of five children, spoke of living with years of abuse. Her small neat house and her calm manner gave no clue as to the story she would tell.

"He drank some when I first met him, but then he drank later. It is not that he drank a lot, it's that he would get very mean and very hateful when he drank. When he would go into one of his rages, I didn't know if I was going to live until the next morning or not. My mind would be clicking—how to keep safe, how to keep the kids safe. I would leave, but then come back. Then I couldn't leave. He threatened to burn my parents' house down. He threatened to shoot them. He said he would shoot the kids or me.

"He beat me and beat the kids. I was afraid to leave. I was afraid to stay. He raped our two daughters and molested the other two. They put him in jail. He is

in the state prison right now. It's been seven years and it feels like another lifetime."

Emily is thirty-three and the mother of four young children. *"After six years of marriage, my husband left me for another woman. Our second child was two months old. I rebounded very quickly and remarried someone I had only known for eight weeks. He was abusive, extremely. It was pure hell. He scared the kids, he scared me. He threatened to kill me. I left, but found out I was pregnant with my third child. I wanted to put the baby up for adoption. I thought she deserved better than she was going to get. I was afraid he would end up hurting her as well.*

"Instead we got back together again, with the baby and my two children, for five months. That's when the real bad stuff happened. I was dragged by the neck across the room, knocked against the wall, punched in the head, had hot pizza dumped on me, all kinds of stuff. I had a broken ankle. I went to the shelter a few times and finally left him. We had a reconciliation attempt that lasted three days and I became pregnant with my fourth child, who is now ten months old. But I am finally free of him."

Carol, thirty-four, dropped out of school in the ninth grade, married, and had a son. *"He was a few years older than me. We went to North Carolina for his job. But he was a hothead and went off on his boss and got fired. He was a wife beater. There was no one to talk to about it. I just dealt with it until I decided I wasn't going to deal with it anymore. When my son was about seven months old I came back here. I got an apartment, went on welfare, and took care of my kid. I was seventeen years old. When I got married I intended it to be forever, but it didn't work out that way."*

Jean, in her early thirties, is the mother of five children. She left her husband after twelve years of marriage. *"He is an alcoholic. When he would drink you couldn't look at him cross-eyed. He would come home and start nitpicking, jumping all over you for nothing. Open your mouth and you might as well make up your mind you are going to get smacked around if you don't keep it shut right. This went on for years and years, and the anger builds up. So finally, we left and came to the shelter."*

Joy, in her early twenties, is not married. The mother of two young children, she described the end of the four-year relationship with their father. *"Three years ago, after my son was born, we split up. He was real abusive. It was okay with my daughter. He was happy with her. When my son came along there was a difference. He was abusive. His father was abusive with him. I wanted to break the cycle up. I didn't want my son to see what he was—to see him hit me. I didn't want a male figure like that for my son."*

LaVerne lived with her child's father for three years. *"Then he got into the drugs, then he got into beating me, and I guess he beat me three times and I was out of there. Since then he has been in and out of jail."*

Leaving the abusive relationship was a positive step in these women's lives. Yet most of them had no skills or job preparation so they could provide for their children. Jean, Gloria, Carol, and Joy had all left high school before graduation. LaVerne is a high school graduate, but has no job skills. With young children and little opportunity to earn money, they were propelled into poverty. Any hope for food and medical care for their children lay with public assistance, at least to get them started.

The stories of Emily and Amelia, who had more education, illustrate the devastating effect of abuse on women and their futures. Emily's four children range in age from ten months to nine years. She had two years of training in art school after high school. Of her attitude before marriage she says, *"I wanted to get married. I didn't know I was going to be working for a living. No one plans to do this. I feel like I am just hanging on the edge. In the past few years its just been one blow after another."*

Amelia has traded the work she loves for safety. She takes whatever work is available in the small town where she now lives, but not much comes up. Right now she needs time to recover. *"Up here it is safe. All I have to do is run out the door and scream for help and everyone would be down. If he did anything to my kids, they would blow him away."*

The Drug- or Alcohol-Addicted Mate

Another frequently mentioned source of betrayal was a mate who used alcohol and drugs excessively, although he might not necessarily have been physically abusive. Marie, in her early thirties and the mother of three children, was separated from her husband. He was going to jail for possession of drugs. *"My husband is a drug addict and an alcoholic. One reason I do not have enough money is because when we were together we had to move so many times, because of him we would get evicted. Every time you move, it costs. One of the reasons I'm having a hard time is because I have these loan and credit card payments.*

"We were separated before, but when I got sick I needed help. At that time he was doing all these drugs. I guess I knew it but I really didn't want to see it. I

just knew I needed someone there to help, but he really wasn't any help anyway."

Vicki, thirty, is divorced with two children. She left her husband when she was twenty-one. *"My husband was one of those that would run around all the time. He drank, which I didn't know because he didn't drink around me. I'm not a drinker. I wasn't aware of all of this until much later. His beer would come first before groceries or anything like that. I was working and paying for the baby-sitter for the two babies. He wouldn't do anything. His booze came first.*

"He would lay around all the time. One day I just up and left. I couldn't take it anymore. Until I got sick and lost my job, I was making it on my own, for nine years. It was very rough, but we did it."

Jessie has four children and was married for twenty years before her divorce a few years ago. *"My husband became a drunk. He was not dependable, I couldn't count on him. He's a Nam vet with problems, in and out of hospitals. He never has any money. He comes to see the children. He is more of a burden to me than a help, but the kids love him and I don't talk him down or anything."*

The Deadbeat Dad

Even without serious addiction problems, some men rarely worked and were supported by the women.

Bobbie: *"When I got married, my husband would not work, so I had to work."*

Susan: *"When our baby was a year and a half old, I went to work at a truck stop and my husband just quit altogether. Then I was trying to raise us. So I left. He is still not working. I guess that will never change."*

Pat is the mother of four young children and in her late twenties. She says of her husband, *"When he was away from us, he would work. But when he was with us he wouldn't work. He didn't think there was a reason for him to work, he enjoyed just being a teenager growing up. He just never hit any type of maturity or responsibility or anything.*

"I did not want the divorce. But I finally realized I would completely drag myself down for life if I didn't get away from him. So I finally got divorced."

Carla, twenty-six, and the mother of three children, the youngest just a year old, lives alone but maintains a relationship with the father of her children. *"He doesn't pay for any of them. He used to when he had a job, but he hasn't been employed for years. His last job was four years ago. He helps out with the child care while I am working. And he'll take them to the park and come over and cook dinner for them if I'm beat."*

The Disappearing Dad

Lastly, some fathers just drop in and out of their children's lives or disappear completely.

Renata, in her late thirties and the mother of two teens, was in and out of a relationship with the children's father for more than twelve years. *"All those years, he didn't pay anything. He would dart in every now and then and dart back out again. He was very abusive mentally. He would tell me that he was everything and that without him I was nothing. He would call me names and say that I was never going to amount to anything. I guess I believed it because I used to say I was leaving him, but I never would.*

"One day I finally realized something was very wrong. I don't have to be treated like this. I am a person. Then I got into the church and getting involved with church activities. I don't see him any more. And I took him to court a few months ago and he is finally paying some child support."

At twenty-one, Anita discovered she was pregnant shortly after she and her boyfriend broke up. *"I didn't have one minute of thinking I wouldn't keep it. I wasn't brought up like that. You just don't do that.*

"The father knows she is here. He saw her when she was two months old. He does not want nothing to do with her. I don't get child support. I don't get anything. I tried to apply, but I don't know his social security number. I have no address. I have nothing. His name is not even in the phone book."

At twenty-nine, Judy, unmarried, has two children with different fathers. *"My oldest child's father is around now. He's been coming down seeing him now. But it took him over nine years. He just started paying child support. I don't know where my daughter's father is. He wasn't working when I knew him. I filed for child support and they are looking for him. But I don't really know if he's in the state."*

Ursula is forty and has three children. Her youngest child has epilepsy. *"I was married the month after I graduated from high school. That was twenty-two years ago. My husband and I were together for seven years. We purchased a home together and then he just left. That was it. He never came back. I don't know where he is. His family don't know where he is. I did sign papers to try to find him. If he really cared about the children he would have come back. He wasn't ready to settle down and really take care of a family."*

While the betrayals took many forms, in all cases the women were left alone to care for and provide for their children. Despite poverty, hardship, and their personal losses and pain, these women remain committed to raising their children. The men may have left or behaved so intolerably that the women were forced to leave, but the children were never left or not cared for.

As Ursula put it, *"I gave birth to these children. I had them because I wanted them, so I took care of them. I will continue to take care of them."* Rather than be castigated by the media and others, these women might well be viewed as heroines. They did not betray their mates or abandon their children. They have remained committed to their families.

The Poverty Equation

The combination of limited education and few job skills, coupled with the husband's or mate's betrayal, is a good predictor of an impoverished life for a woman and her children. Her limited education and training place her in low-level jobs that do not provide sufficient income to raise two or three children. Even when a woman is able to provide for her family, the slightest problem—a sick child, the mother's illness, a factory closing—easily moves the struggling family back into poverty. It is not that a woman cannot survive without a male. Divorced or separated women with sufficient job skills and a good job history, especially those with college degrees and careers can, albeit with great difficulty, provide for their children alone. But it is the woman with minimal job skills training, in a work world that already discriminates against women, who finds herself in poverty and is forced to rely on public assistance.

The mate's betrayal and his own limited employment opportunities are a significant part of the poverty equation. Families suffering with domestic violence and alcohol and drug addiction have wounds that need healing. Children in these families may have symptoms, such as anger and overreacting in school, that exacerbate the child-rearing process. A woman leaving an abusive relationship usually does so with her self-esteem in need of bolstering at the very time that she needs to be self-confident in order to do well in the employment search. The man's difficulties have usually depleted what funds the family had or made it almost impossible to save any money.

Financially, as these women's voices reveal, child support was usually not available or of such a small amount that it didn't help very much. And in almost all cases, this support came as a result of a court order, not as voluntary contributions to the child's welfare. Many men live chaotic lives, not willing or not able to support their own children.

The married women, in particular, seem to have entered the relationships in good faith. But the men were not dependable. Rather than finding a partner, the women experienced either a relationship involving abuse or requiring them to be their mate's financial supporter.

Early Years: Stories of Survivors

There is a third factor—early years and family influences—that was a problem for some of the women. Some experienced abuse early in their lives. Some had alcoholic parents or parents who died when the women were young. Others were raised in households that fostered a sense of unworthiness and low self-esteem.

Julie recounted a childhood of abuse and parental addiction. *"My step-father was an alcoholic. My mother was trying for martyrdom and still is. I was taught by my family that being you are a woman, you are dumb. You have no rights. When my uncle was sexually abusing me, he said that was his right. I can remember always being told, 'You are dumb. You will never amount to a hill of beans. If you amount to anything, it will be a whore. You are no good.' Even now, if I tell them about my going back to school, they say, 'You can't do that. You are out of your mind to try that.'*

"We were very poor. The school was no help. I can remember one time in the third grade going to school, the back of my legs had welts on them. The teacher wanted to report my family, but she was told, 'You cannot. It is a family matter.' The only help I got was from the church ladies. I remember them wiping our noses. Here we are, we have these crew-cut haircuts, our noses are running. I mean, it's not clear, it's green, you know. We are dirty and these women are wiping our noses, they are telling us we are special. They were my lifeline. I wanted to be like those ladies."

Leona, forty years old, also told of a childhood of abuse and mistreatment. *"I'm the oldest of eight children. When my mother left us, my father gave us to people he knew. I did a lot of cooking, cleaning, dressing for my brothers and sisters and my foster parents' family.*

"My stepbrothers, they used to come into my room at night and touch me and stuff. When I used to tell my stepmother about it, she would tell me, 'Oh, now, you are just letting them.' They blamed me.

"My family used to call me dumb, stupid, ignorant. 'Oh you make me sick, get out of my face.' Things like that."

Eva, an energetic twenty-two-year-old, also told the story of a survivor. *"My mom and dad were divorced when I was two. My mom got remarried when I was five. My stepfather used to beat on her, but I didn't really understand what was going on. I would go in my room and cry and stuff. As I got older I found out what was going on. I wanted to protect my mom.*

"She kicked me out over him when I was twelve. I stabbed him a couple of times and ripped his eyelid and stuff. He was hurting her and I jumped on him for that and put him in the hospital. He wasn't on drugs or anything, he was just mean. She kicked me out over that because she was scared.

"They are divorced now and she is sorry. I don't like to see a man beating on any woman. That's part of why I want to be a cop. I want to get those guys."

Susan, twenty-two, describes a nonsupportive early family life that continues today. *"My father ran out when my mom was six months pregnant with me and my brother was two and a half years old. I've never seen him in my life. She raised me and my brother on welfare.*

"She is always telling me I'll never be nothing. 'You'll never do this and you'll never do that. You can't be this and you can't be that,' is all she says. When I tried to move out on my own, she said, 'Well, I don't have a daughter.'

"She can't be down on my back dragging me down all the time. I've come too far to have somebody drag me down, even if it is my own mother."

Arlene, thirty-four, described an early traumatic event and her attempts to overcome its effects. Although she described events that happened over sixteen years ago, she was visually nervous and cried a few times as she talked. *"I was married at fifteen and my daughter was born when I was sixteen. I left school but I went back. I took two grades together to catch up and I was the only one who finished high school out of twelve kids. We were very poor growing up.*

"When I was eighteen a family member asked me to do something and I did it without thinking. It was a criminal act and I was convicted. I served some time at the end of my eleventh grade. I had to go back to school in my senior year. I then had to serve more time in the winter. I went back and worked twice as hard. I served five months. I had a tutor in prison and I was on the honor roll. But it was very hard for me to go back and face my classmates. I made it through my senior year by the skin of my teeth.

"There was no one in my family to influence us to continue our education. I have always expected the worst. I think I told myself I didn't deserve any better

because of the way I was raised. My father made us feel like that, you know, made us feel small.

"*The prison record has caused a lot of self-esteem problems for me. For a long time I was afraid to look for a job. Whenever I went out job hunting and had to fill out that application, the question was always there, 'Have you ever been convicted?' I don't like people getting to know me too well because I don't want to tell them about that part of my life. I didn't tell my daughter, who is now eighteen, until a few months ago about my prison record.*"

Not all women had negative early experiences or nonsupportive families. Some women spoke of warm relationships with their families.

Ursula: "*I had a beautiful childhood. My parents took care of me even though they were separated. I saw both of my parents and enjoyed life. I enjoy being around my family.*"

Anita: "*My mom, dad, sisters, and brothers were all there when my daughter was born. Everyone was very excited and very supportive.*"

Most of the women, however, did come from very poor families or families with very limited financial resources. As Arlene describes it, "*We all had rough lives. Nobody in my family has a lot of money so I haven't really been able to turn to other family members to borrow money or anything like that.*" Regardless of a positive or negative childhood, when the woman was placed in the position of being the head of the household, her family was rarely able to provide any financial help.

Poverty and the Single Mother

This chapter has presented the ABC's of poverty for the single mother. An absence of requisite education and job training; betrayal by the mate, often cruel and painful in form, and in some cases abusive; and neglectful and nonsupportive family backgrounds are elements of the poverty equation.

FOUR. Women of Commitment

*Struggling with the
Mother-Provider Dilemma*

Poor single mothers are women of commitment. Despite all that happens to them—poverty, loss, broken dreams—they remain committed to their children. The men may leave, but the women do not leave their children. They try to forge a life for the children and for themselves. To do this, they have to grapple with the dilemma of balancing work demands and family needs. They have to be both the mother and the provider.

Think of the mother and provider roles as two ends of a seesaw: no matter what position it is in, the woman has a difficult time. All of her decisions are trade-offs. If circumstances prevent an active provider role, so that the mothering end of the seesaw is tipped up, the minimal or absent provider role means abject poverty. If it is tipped up the opposite way, so that the provider role is dominant, the strain on the mother role produces problems and loss for the children. Balancing the two is complicated under any circumstances.

Trying to balance the two with scarce financial resources is a daily challenge, full of stresses, strains, and uncertainties. The women struggle with it all, knowing that there are no other choices for them. The reliable and dependable mate seems a crushed dream. There is no child support, or it is not sufficient to reduce the strain of providing and to enhance the mothering role. For most of the women, a job with flexibility to ease the strain of parenting and furnish a high-enough income to ease the stress of providing is not possible without further education and training.

Through the Lens of Motherhood

Of all the study's outcomes, the most prominent was the priority of the women: they are mothers first. They view the world through the lens of motherhood. Work and all decisions related to it are placed within the context of their role and responsibility as a mother. They do not see themselves as providers, struggling to be the parent within that context. Rather, they view themselves as mothers, and struggle to be providers within *that* context.

The priority of motherhood reveals itself in many different ways. For a few, motherhood is the only available option. Their children's health or other problems require a full-time presence. For most of the others, the way they grapple with and feel about the work-family dilemma reflects their priority of motherhood.

No Choice—My Child Needs Me

Carol, thirty-four, recounts a time when, on her way to further education, her child's needs made it necessary to put that dream on hold. *"My youngest son was starting school, and I was pregnant with my daughter. I was going to school for my GED. I had her during Christmas break and went right back. They had a day care on the premises, which made it real easy for me to go to classes. I left her downstairs and went upstairs to complete my classes. Otherwise I would not have been able to do it. There was nobody that I was going to leave my three-week-old baby with.*

"Then after I completed the courses, she was about a year and a half, she burned her right arm. She had second- and third-degree burns on her arm. It was back and forth, sometimes two or three times a week to the doctors. I didn't have no time for school then. I was glad I had completed the one thing and not yet started in anything else. I just put everything else on hold to take care of her.

"She was so little. There was no one there to help me. I was scared a lot because I never dealt with burns. I felt like, 'Oh, God, what am I doing?' She would cry when I had to change the bandages. You feel like you are pulling the skin off or something the way she is screaming. It was a terrible time. But I made it this far. I keep trying to make it more."

Ursula's husband left her shortly before the birth of their third child. *"My daughter had problems when she was first born. She only weighed four pounds, three ounces. I was so afraid I was going to lose her. I had to take care of her, I loved her. It is a gift from God.*

"After she was born I couldn't work anymore. She was sick constantly. She had problems holding down milk. Her motor skills weren't very good. She couldn't use her hands too well. They didn't pick up on her seizures until she was three.

"All the years she was growing up, I couldn't work. You never knew when she would get sick. If she had a seizure in school someone had to pick her up. I couldn't give that responsibility to someone else. She is my responsibility. I would never know when she was going to get sick. It might be today. It might be tomorrow. She might get sick for two days straight or she might not get sick for another week. Would a boss understand that? If the seizures happened at night, I might be up all night. If they were violent, I would be in the hospital all night. You don't want to go to work the next day half dragging in. I've tried to get her under control, to the best of my ability. She hasn't been sick for a year. Now it's time for me to venture out so I can take care of myself and take care of her."

Marilyn, in her early thirties, completed the tenth grade. Her youngest child, now eight, needs constant supervision. *"My now former husband tried to slit his wrists, just to get us to come back. My son seen this. Then, he started, whenever he didn't get his own way, he would take a fork and say he was going to kill himself. My son was hospitalized for two months, and now he's on medication.*

"He's a lot better since I am away from his daddy. He used to yell and scream and fight and kick. He got suspended in kindergarten. But I can't find anyone who will baby-sit. I live with my parents, but my mother wouldn't want me to go to the store for a minute. I need someone who can handle him, somebody who's got a firm hand, yet at the same time knows when to be gentle. It would have to be individual care, but I don't have the money for that. So except for school, we are together all the time. I get in the bathtub and he's right there. He wants in, too. I can't even take a bath alone."

For these women, for either long or short periods of time, being the provider was not possible. Carol was finally able to return to school and recently completed a dental technician's program. Ursula's daughter is nearing high school graduation and Ursula is ready and looking forward to going out on her own in the work world. Marilyn is still struggling. For these women, public assistance was or is their only means of support. Ursula called it a lifeline.

Emily, thirty-three, also feels that motherhood is her only option, but for somewhat different reasons. Despite needing to work, she has difficulty seeing herself in any role except that of mother. Emily was deserted by her first husband and abused by her second. She cares for her four children, who range in age from ten months to nine years.

"The only thing I can really do is the four kids. I do them really well because I put them first. I've always felt that staying at home is what I wanted to do while they were little. I want to give them what they need because their lifestyles have been so uprooted. I don't know how to do both. I feel they come first, before work, before anything else. Yet I need to eventually get out and work for them. There's no balance yet. They bring me great joy. But because of all they have gone through, they need so much of me."

In other circumstances, Emily's choice would be applauded. Her four young children come first, and she is more than willing to put her needs and aspirations on hold in order to devote her time and energies to them. Sitting with Emily in her small but neat apartment, you could easily envision her in a large home, enjoying the Brownies or Girl Scouts, and spending time with her four very young children. But she knows she must someday, soon, take on the role of provider and find a way to be the mother and the provider.

Flexibility—At a Price

For many of the women, making motherhood a priority is reflected by their attempts to develop working arrangements that allow them time with their children. They work, but are women who want to be mothers first.

Anita, who is working, is a woman who is trying to give her daughter all the benefits of a full-time mother. A vibrant woman in her mid-twenties, her top priority is to be a good mother. Anita's small, cheery apartment, which she painted herself, reflects that love and priority. The one bedroom, occupied by her five-year-old daughter, was pink and the bed was filled with dolls and stuffed animals, presents from her mother's ten siblings. Anita, never married and a high school graduate, works as a waitress. This job allows her the flexibility and scheduling she needs in order to spend time with her daughter. *"I've been on county assistance since I was pregnant. I had a medical card. I get a medical card for her and I get food stamps. Other than that, we don't receive anything. Her medical card covers everything, from the dentist to the doctor. If it wasn't for them, I wouldn't be able to do it, to tell you the truth. I also have Section 8 housing. It goes by my income. If my income goes up, then my portion of the rent goes up.*

"I waitress. I have always waitressed. I have been a waitress since I was sixteen. I work three days a week. I don't want to work any more than that until she is in first grade. But I also want to go back to school. I want to get into computers. When I'm at work, my sister baby-sits for me. So it works out well.

"Sometimes the money gets a little tight. You just make do with what you have. I don't get no child support, you know. Not anything. I don't get no help at all from him. The only reason I don't work full-time is that she needs to know I am here, because he isn't here. She needs to know she has me to depend on. If she needs me, I am here. But I don't want to be a waitress all my life. When she goes to first grade, I would really like to go back to school. I could take classes during the day and still work my three days a week. That way, I'm in school when she is in school. I don't believe in your child going to school all day, and you work at night and then on weekends. When do you see them? Once she starts first grade and is in school all day, I will have to change. Right now I have all morning to spend with her and during the week I have the evenings to spend with her. So I have plenty of time. But once she starts first grade, I won't. So I need to decide what I really want to do. It might take me five or six years until I really get a good pattern, but it is going to be worth it in the long run."

LaVerne, thirty-four, unmarried with one child, also works a limited schedule. She would prefer to work more, but there are few, if any, available jobs. *"I was fired from my job because my daughter was sick. So I had to go on assistance, mainly so my daughter could have medical assistance. Now I only receive food stamps and some help with my rent.*

"I cut hair. I work Thursday, Friday, and Saturday. I love my job. My daughter is in school during the day. When she is finished, she walks down to the shop and stays there with me. On Saturdays, the lady upstairs keeps her. I'd like to work more hours, but it takes so long for your clientele to build up. I'm trying to get another part-time job here at the nursing home.

"Having my daughter around, it's like my right arm having her here. When she ain't around, you are looking for her. I take her to school every day and I

pick her up, except on Thursdays and Fridays when she walks to the shop. But even then she walks with the other kids and the shop is close to the school."

Marie works thirty hours a week as a file clerk and has three children under twelve. She receives food stamps and subsidized help with child care and utilities. She gets no child support. Marie plans to go full-time soon, but worries about its impact on her life.

"When I first started I was full-time. Then after I had my third child it got so hectic I decided to go part-time. First it was three days a week. Then I switched to five days a week at six hours a day to go with the kids' school schedule. So after seven years, I make $8.33 per hour, but it just doesn't pay the bills for all four of us.

"I like being a mother. I like spending time with them and taking them out. I like to go to the playground and I like reading them stories. It's just plain hard. That's all I can say. I try to keep them active and in activities, like band, wrestling, and baton. It's so much rushing around for me. But I want to steer my children in the right direction. I want to see them do more with their life than I did."

Marie's $8.33 hourly wage comes to approximately $12,995 per year. This is still under the 1993 U.S. poverty threshold of $14,705 for a family of four. Although still poor, Marie is actually more fortunate than many of the other women. A half-time job of twenty hours a week, at $5 an hour, slightly above minimum wage, would bring in around $100 per week or $5,200 per year. Even at full-time hours, wages of $5 an hour amount to only about $10,400 in annual income.

Not all of the women who want to fit work hours around time with their children are able to do so. Jessie has four children, two still at home of elementary school age. She is looking for work, but she has limited job skills and the area has few jobs.

"I need to work during the day so I can be here with my kids at night. Minimum-wage pay and an evening job where I would have to pay a baby-sitter is not worth it. It's more trouble than it's worth and in the long run I would be making out worse. They would take away my medical and my food stamps and my kids would lose me.

"My kids are first. My kids are always first. Basically everything I work for or think of working for is around them—what's best for them. The hours, the pay, the kind of work I do—all the decisions revolve around them.

"My husband was a drunk. He would be passed out somewhere and the kids would be sneaking out a window and climbing down a tree and going off

with some boy. That's when I chose to stay home for a couple of years. I had no one to take care of the home front.

"My kids were always more important to me than anything. They needed me so that's why I stayed home. Then when you get out of the work field for a couple of years, it is hard to get back in. Your applications say up until such and such a year, there is nothing, no job history. They look at that and say '. . . um.' "

For these mothers the problem with flexible arrangements or in seeking jobs compatible with children's schedules is that there is no dad in the background who is helping to pay the bills. Moreover, the jobs they are able to get do not pay very much. So the price they pay for their priorities is a high one. Every hour not worked is a financial sacrifice. But it is an important and perhaps necessary one. They feel they need to be with their children since there is no dad to share the parenting role. There is no other parent to pick up the slack.

For Anita, LaVerne, and Marie, the only way to offset the financial loss is public assistance. They don't get much help—food stamps, medical benefits, help with housing or utilities. But it is enough to just make it and still be there for the children. And they don't like it. Marie and LaVerne both commented on how degrading it is to go to the supermarket with food stamps. Proud women, they each stated, "but I work," yet they felt the stares from other shoppers when they used the stamps. As LaVerne said, *"You gotta do what you gotta do. I have a child to take care of and if I have to do that to take care of her, then I'm going to do it."*

Ironically, the women's commitment to their children does not produce praise. Rather, they are often erroneously perceived as being uncommitted workers. Yet, if all the circumstances of their lives were considered, they might more correctly be perceived as women of commitment, placing a high priority on the welfare of their children.

Being the Provider

Some of the women were on their way toward jobs with the financial ability to lift them and their families out of poverty. They expressed pride in their efforts and recognized the value of being the provider, while also expressing the pain of spending less time with their children.

Susan, twenty-two, has a son in kindergarten. She recently began work as a trained nurse's aide and plans to continue in the nursing field. *"The hardest thing about it is that I don't have time like I used to. I used to be here all day with him. When he went to Head Start last fall, I was here to put him on the bus. I was here to get him off the bus. Mom's not here all the time for every little problem, for every little cut.*

"I was thinking, 'Do I want to be a full-time mother or a full-time nurse?' It doesn't seem like you have the time to be both. It's either one or the other. But we manage pretty well. We have his time before he goes to school. That's our time now."

Hard Choices, Few Choices

In varying degrees, the work-family dilemma is one faced by working mothers across all income levels. Making motherhood a priority is not unique to this group of women. The difference is the circumstances that limit the options available to poor single mothers. They lack a mate who can furnish either financial or parenting support, just as they lack the education and training to find jobs to provide an adequate income or enough money to "buy out" some aspects of parenting. For poor single mothers, a difference in degree becomes a difference in kind.

The Balancing Act: Stresses and Strains

Lowering the mother-only end of the seesaw and raising the provider end increases the daily stresses and strains of life. How do these women balance work and family? What kind of schedules do they have, especially when their options are so few? What kind of arrangements do they make when money is so tight?

Some Schedules

Judy, with a nine-year-old son and a baby, will soon be returning to work as a waitress. *"I will work from six in the morning until 2 PM every day. My mom will watch the baby, get my boy off the school bus, and then I'll be home. I got to get up about four in the morning to get to my job and will get home around 3:30 PM. Then I'll get dinner, play with the baby, and help my son with homework."*

Connie, twenty-seven, works part-time, takes college classes, and has two children in elementary school. *"In the mornings, I have a teenager who lives next door. I pay her to help me to get them ready, so I can leave an hour earlier.*

In the afternoons the kids are by themselves from 4 PM until 5:30 PM. They can walk home from school. They have my number and I call them. They come in, lock the door, and no one is allowed in. I don't leave them alone for more than two hours. At night I have a class, which is tough. I try to take day classes when I can. Other nights we have Girl Scouts or they have their church class."

Jean has five children and works at a food-processing plant. *"When I started, the time was 7 AM. It was understood when I started that my children go to the day care from 6:30 AM until 5:30 PM, that I could not possibly come in earlier than seven and stay past five. If I get there late, I'm charged seventy cents per minute per child for any time past 5:30. I have three of them registered there. The five-year-old is there all day, and the ten- and eleven-year-old go before and after school.*

"Anyway, they changed the starting time to 6 AM and we have to stay until we are finished, even if it's after 5 PM. You stay or you are terminated. This is new. My neighbor is going to take the three little kids at 5:30 in the morning so I can get to work at 6 AM. That means we will be getting up around 4:30 AM. She will take them to the day care, and if I'm not back to get them before 5:30, she is going to get them. My twelve- and thirteen-year-old are on their own.

"The company really didn't give me any choice. I am trying to find another job."

Carla, twenty-six, with three young children including an infant, describes how she feels about working and raising children at the same time. *"After you get off from work, you got to come home and you have to cook and clean and take care of the kids, and that's always hard too. Sometimes you get so tired. Just taking care of the children plus working is hard. Whether you have one or five, it's hard. It was hard when I had one, it's even harder with three. My oldest, she's eleven, she helps out a lot. My other child tries to help out. But, it's just surviving, I guess."*

Pat, twenty-seven, with four children, expressed similar thoughts. *"It is very difficult for me, as far as doing everything by myself. You are the mommy, you take care of the house, and you take care of the bills, you take care of everyone at home."*

Off Balance: I Miss My Mom

There is no comfortable balance for these single mothers, since the children will always prefer a full-time mother, especially since there is no father in the picture. Some of the children are understanding.

Julie: *"When I finished school, my kids were tickled to death. Mom would no longer be stressed out. We will have a normal mom, a mom who doesn't have her nose in a book until one or two in the morning studying. A mom that will be there for us, because I wasn't always able to be there for them, because of my class schedule, because of studying. They were thrilled and I think they are starting to see the light at the end of the tunnel for us."*

But other women reported strong negative reactions from their children when they devoted full time to work or school or both.

Sally, thirty-seven, worked full-time for two years in a restaurant. She did a variety of jobs, including waitressing and inventory, and often worked overtime. *"I was working full-time in a restaurant. I liked the job. There was one thing I regretted about working there and that was my long hours. It took me away from my family and that did some damage. Me and my daughter grew apart instead of closer. She was about thirteen.*

"We sat down and talked about it. She thought my job was more important than my family. That hurt. I tried to tell her so that she would understand, my son, too. I tried to tell them the only reason I was working was so that they would have a better life."

Pat works full-time as a paralegal and her children are reacting negatively to this new job. *"They have come right out and told me how I have abandoned them by working and not being at home with them. Whenever something happens—'You weren't here, Mommy. It's your fault.'"*

Returning to School

For most of the women, climbing out of poverty means not just starting the long road of education and training, but doing it as mothers with little or no money.

Carla spoke of her failed attempt to get her high school diploma when her two children were preschoolers. *"They have a program here where instead of getting your GED you can go back and get your diploma. You start out with how many credits you had when you quit. I needed a lot of credits. It probably would have taken me two years in the program to finish.*

"I started out, but then I quit. It was too hard with the work and then at nighttime going to school and then coming home with the kids. It got so that I couldn't do it. So, I had to make a choice, and of course I have to work, so I let the school go.

"But one day I'll go back and get my GED. It will be something at least I can tell the kids. That okay, I might have quit, but I did go back. If I can make that choice again, I would've never quit."

Getting the Diploma: A Difficult Journey

There were four women in the study who did not quit, but went on to obtain an associate college degree. All four had just finished their programs of study, and two were recently employed and two were actively looking. Managing both school and family was difficult for all of them. With minimal financial resources, they had to rely on a patchwork of child-care assistance. As parents, their children's needs had to be balanced against the demands of school, work, and travel time. As single women, they usually had to do it all themselves—the worry and the work. Finally, their own anxieties about success and failure in their new undertaking often took a backseat to just trying to juggle it all.

Arlene, the mother of three, had two elementary-school-age children at home when she returned to school. *"I just got my degree in business management from a local business college and accepted a job offer last week with a bank. There were so many times I felt so impatient and got so discouraged. I felt like I wasn't going to get anywhere. But now my goals are just around the corner, I'm getting there.*

"It took me two years to finish my program. I also had a part-time job. Somedays I would go from here to Hallers for a class, then to Telmont for my job, then back over to Hallers for more classes and then home. Those were the longest, hardest days, when I had tight schedules like that. I had like three night classes in a row and it was hard on me. My schedule was so hectic. I didn't have time to see my family. It was really hard.

"One automobile problem could set me back a couple of months. I was set back so many times, sometimes I just sit back and I am amazed I made it through. My sister helped out with the baby-sitting. She would pick them up from day care, feed them supper, and give them baths. Then she would bring them to my house, put them to bed, and wait for me to get home, usually around 9:30 PM. I really owe her so much."

Julie also returned to school when her children were very young. She recently received her degree in computer applications. *"When I started school my children were three and five. It was like a three-ring circus. I was carrying five classes, taking care of two children, one with a learning disability, trying to juggle my schedule, her schedule, and her sister's schedule.*

"On Mondays, Wednesdays, and Fridays, I was doing two and three trips a day. I had a 7:30 AM, 9:00 AM, 1:00 PM, and 2:30 PM class. We would get up at 5:30 AM, I would take them to day care at 6:30 and I would be on the road by 7 AM.

"I would come back home at 11:00 AM, get something to eat, get supper started, go back for my 1:00 PM and then I had a 2:30 PM class so I didn't get home and pick my children up until 4:30 or 5 PM. On Tuesdays and Thursdays I only had one class, so you kind of could catch your breath.

"Every term was different, but it was all juggling. Cars would break down, class schedules wouldn't match. It was hard to find baby-sitters. I also started teaching labs.

"When I finished, it was like fireworks and cotton candy and the whole nine yards."

Two of the four women, Pat and Gloria, have traveled a very long road. They first had to get their GEDs before moving on to higher education. Pat was fifteen and finishing the tenth grade when she left high school. She completed her GED when she was in her early twenties, the divorced mother of three young children. She then decided to pursue a college degree.

"The first year of college was all day classes. The three children were in school and day care and it worked out. But at the end of the first semester I was pregnant. So I drove back and forth, while I was pregnant, for two semesters. My mother helped out with the baby-sitting.

"The second year it was harder. It was mostly night classes, but they had nighttime child care. I worked with that and baby-sitters, but it's hard to find sitters at night. Baby-sitters want to baby-sit during the day. My mother wasn't able to anymore.

"There were a lot of complications with the baby. I was surprised that I got back to college with him being just a couple of weeks old. I would come home at night and study. He never seemed to sleep. He screamed and cried all night and all day, so it was difficult, to say the least."

Gloria completed the eleventh grade and then dropped out. Seven years ago, following the imprisonment of her abusive husband, she went on public assistance. She completed her GED and then considered further education. Her five children ranged in age from fourteen to twenty-two when she started work toward her associate degree at a business college.

"It was scary going back to school. I was forty. But it wasn't so bad. Everyone treated me okay.

"I went full-time, five days a week. My youngest was fourteen, so the kids helped me. They took care of a lot of the housework and cooking. Most of the

weekends I shut myself in the bedroom to do my schoolwork and they more or less took care of a lot of things. It was hard when the work got tough, when the kids acted up, when the car broke down, when we had no money.

"It took me two years. I am proud that a woman my age could make a 3.8."

Women of Commitment

The strain of multiple roles cannot be underestimated. Parents in dual-career marriages find it tough going, juggling jobs and children. How much harder it is for women alone trying to be both mother and provider. They are often forced into a catch-22 situation. The maximum scheduling flexibility they can find is usually in dead-end jobs, such as waitressing. In the short run, these jobs allow them time to be with their children. But in the long run, they will never improve their financial situation. They will just keep working harder.

Returning to school for further education offers hope for a better financial future. The voices here speak to the tremendous amount of effort and energy it takes to do so successfully. "It was hard" is perhaps the best summary of their stories. Once employed, their financial pressures will lessen. But the stresses and strains of being both the provider and the mother will continue.

The women are committed to building a better life for themselves and their children. They do not give up, in spite of hardships, poverty, hassles, and fatigue. They face the daily grind, the deadening routine, the day with insufficient hours, or the next "emergency" that will eat up their meager money supply. They keep going, despite uncertain tomorrows. Each step forward is an heroic act.

Why do they do it? What keeps them going? To a woman, the answer was always "my children."

Gloria: *"My children kept me from giving up. I've never been the type of person for suicide, but if it wouldn't have been for the kids, I think I would have given up. When I was in that [abusive] situation I couldn't see no end to it. They made me strong because I had to be strong for them."*

Bobbie: *"My kids. Without them I would be dead by now. I think about them and I keep myself straight."*

Carla: *"One day I was putting a tent together and my daughter looks at me and says, 'Mom, do you know what, you're special.' It's times like that—after I've stayed up with them, hours and hours, they are screaming and crying. Little things like that one sentence, 'Mom, you're special,' can make up for all the times when you just thought you were going to go nuts."*

For these women, the pressure of being both mother and provider is wearing. But without a father able or willing to provide for his children, these women shoulder both roles, or try to do so. If they are able to perform well as providers, sometimes their own children are angry with them, and sometimes they are angry with themselves for not being able to be there for the kids when they are needed. With their limited education and job skills, their provider efforts often don't meet the family needs, so public assistance becomes necessary. They are continually in no-win situations, yet they carry on. They are women of commitment.

FIVE. **Stone Soup**

Single Parenting in Poverty

These impoverished single mothers are called on to make a family life out of almost nothing. Poverty is the stage on which their dramas unfold. It has very few props. The women struggle to raise their children with minimal resources beyond the basics of shelter and food, and even food supplies sometimes run low. In addition, the ghost of the absent father is present, adding to the negative circumstances the women must deal with. The ghost is in the scars that an abusive or addicted father has left on the children. Or the ghost is the empty space in the children's lives that the women work hard to fill up. Their lives are like stone soup—trying to make a lot out of very little.

Living in Poverty

The average income for the women in the interview sample is $7,802 per year. Slightly more than half of the women are on full county assistance, which includes a cash grant, food stamps, and a medical card. Most of the others work part-time, but still receive food stamps and some medical benefits. Some women receive help with other expenses, such as heating. Two women are, or are about to be, employed full-time.

Total Support

Julie, divorced, with two young children, has been living on full benefits for three years. *"I receive $396 a month from the state. My husband pays $160 a month child support and I get $50 a month of that as a rebate from the state. That's the same budget I've been on all this time. Sometimes you rob Peter to pay Paul and pray Paul is not broke. It's very tight. There is $280 coming out of there for rent. That doesn't leave much to pay for heat, phone, and everything else.*

"I'm still waiting for subsidized housing. I do get heat assistance, which is like $183 per winter. That doesn't last long because this house is old. It is gas heat. I use $60 a month for December, January, and February and pray that March is not too cold.

"I worry that the bills won't get paid because I'm very prideful. It is some worry—the money. We've got a roof over our head and we do have food in our belly. It's just the money—when you think that we are living on really $4,000 per year. There is no money there.

"The best example I can give you about money is I can't go in a store and buy my kids a pack of gum without worrying about where the money is coming from. Fifty-nine cents isn't a lot of money to most people. To me, that's a lot of money. I can buy something else with that fifty-nine cents that they need."

Jessie, thirty-nine and divorced, with two children at home, has also been on full benefits for three years. *"I get $182.50 every two weeks from the state, plus food stamps and the medical. I couldn't make it without the medical. The money is barely enough for rent and utilities.*

"I pay $200 in rent. It's not subsidized. I keep one whole check out and some of the next check for the rent. That doesn't leave much for utility bills, much less when the kids need books for school and stuff or even clothes. I don't get any child support.

"Last winter was rough. We couldn't use wood because the chimney wasn't working right. We get fuel assistance, but they only help you so much—about

two times. That got me through to January. I still had the end of January, February, and March. It was still cold. We have a kerosene heater and we pretty much close off the house and stay in one room. We all sleep in that room and when we are home we stay in that room."

Partial Help

Jean was on full benefits for a year. She earned her GED during that period and is now working part-time. For the last several months she and her five school-age children have been living on her earnings, although she still receives food stamps and a medical card.

"I'm proud of myself. I'm not getting no forty hours a week down there at the plant, but I'm managing. I'm managing to keep the bills caught up and everything."

Marie, with three children under twelve, works thirty hours a week and receives food stamps and a temporary medical card. *"I gross $499 every two weeks. I net $329, that's $658 per month. I'm on subsidized day care, which is $36 a month, and subsidized rent, which is $68 a month. I get some help on electric and heat. There's not much left for everything else like clothes, telephone, gas, shampoo, my loan. But I'm a bargain hunter. I shop at Goodwill and I go to the Rescue Mission."*

When Things Get Really Tough

Many of the women said that by the end of the month they are sometimes out of food or money. They are forced to borrow, rely on local charities, or juggle their bills in order to feed themselves and their children and make ends meet.

Marie: *"Usually by the end of the month, before the food stamps come in, I am out of everything. I go to the Food Pantry and they will give me a box and a bag of groceries. If you use up all of your crisis money for heat, you can go to the Salvation Army and they will help you out with fifty dollars.*

"I don't like to ask people for help. I usually wait until the last minute. Only if I absolutely have to have something, then I will swallow my pride. Last week I had to ask my dad for help. I called and said, 'Would you please help me get my son a pair of sneakers?'"

Jessie: *"You always run out of food stamps by the end of the month. That is when you go to the Food Basket and the Catholic Church. They help a lot, they really do. My mom tries to help, too. It is tough.*

"I've looked for every possible source of help. The Food Basket and the Catholic Church help with food and clothes. Lutheran Social Services will help with heat. Children's Aid will help with clothes and toys at Christmas.

"I'm existing. When I look back, I don't know how we made it through last month. But here we are."

Renata has two teenagers. She has held a variety of full-time jobs, but is currently on full benefits. *"I don't do too bad, except for things like bread or milk. If I run low, I ask my mother for something. She will give it to me and I replace it back to her when I get my food stamps."*

Carla works part-time as a telemarketer to support her three children, ranging from an infant to one in sixth grade.

"I worry about the bills that are coming in that I don't have the money to pay for. The bill collectors call you on the phone. I'll say, 'Okay, I'll try.' But if I don't send it in, they keep calling back. I would like to be able to pay my bills on time but sometimes there just isn't any money."

Raising Children in Poverty: The Pain of Not Providing

For almost all of the women, the most painful part of these tight budgets is not being able to provide well for their children. Finding the money for basics is difficult. Going to the movies or a fast-food restaurant usually costs too much money. Yet, rarely, if ever, did a woman mention items, such as a new dress or a trip, that she might want. Her energies are focused on providing the basics of shelter, food, and clothing for her family. If she can manage all of this reasonably well, she feels okay. For her, the pain of poverty is what her children cannot have.

Basic Needs

Even some of the most basic things, such as shoes and school supplies, pose financial dilemmas for these single mothers.

Jessie: *"My daughter was crying the other day. She doesn't usually talk about what is bothering her. But that day she did. She said, 'I'm tired of being poor.'*

"The book fair is this week. They want to buy books and I don't have the money to give them. Little things like that really bother me bad. They really eat at me. All their friends can do it, but they can't. All I can tell them is that I don't have the money."

Julie: *"The hardest part of being poor is to see them want, even if it is just a Slinky, and knowing that you can't provide that Slinky."*

Joy, twenty-four, has two preschool children. *"They need beds now. They have cribs, but they are almost out of them. But I have to wait and lay away and pick prices, when they need them now. That's the hard part of it."*

Marie: *"It's hard to explain money problems to children. When they say, 'I need shoes, I need clothes,' and you got to keep telling them, 'You have to wait, just wait.' I know the shoes he has on are ready to fall off his feet."*

Renata: *"It's hard not to get my kids the different things they need. I try to get it, but sometimes it takes a little longer. So far, they understand that if I can't get it right then, if they wait a while, I'll try to get it."*

LaVerne, who has one child, works part-time. *"It's hard to say 'no' to my daughter all the time. 'No, you can't have this. No, you can't have that.' Then they send home book papers from school. She wants to buy books from the school. I don't have five dollars to send to the school for a book. That's kind of upsetting."*

Doing Without: Just Living Is Hard

Just living is hard in poverty. The women and their children are surrounded by places, like restaurants, and events, like local fairs, to which they can't go because there is no money. Holiday presents are few or sometimes nonexistent.

Amelia, who lives in a small town, describes what she does with her two children. *"The hardest is trying to take my children places they want to go. I can't afford it. It's that simple.*

"There was a fair here three weeks ago, but there wasn't any money for the tickets. I put the window up and we could hear the music and the rides. We walked over there and watched the rides going. I thought, 'Oh, my God, this hurts.'

"They built a new restaurant here on the corner, a fast-food place. But I haven't been able to take them because I don't have the money. I told the kids— the monies will come in, then the rent and the bills go first. Then you guys go second, all the school stuff and supplies you need. Then, whatever is left over is for entertainment. Let me tell you, there is nothing left."

Carla, living in a city, experiences similar difficulties. *"My kids say, 'Mom, we feel like going out to eat tonight' or 'we want to do this or that.' I would like to have the money to say, 'Okay we'll go,' instead of saying, 'Well, we can't this*

*week,' or 'we can't next week.' I just keep putting it off, but there is never any
extra money for such things."*

Holidays, such as Christmas and birthdays, were mentioned frequently as
especially painful because of the lack of extra money.

Jessie: *"Christmas coming up this year is a scary thing. I told them
yesterday—maybe we should just skip Christmas this year. Maybe put it off
until June. They are at the age when they know there is no Santa Claus. They
know it depends on me. It's real tough when they believe in Santa Claus
because they don't care if you are working or not. I would like to believe in
Santa Claus again myself."*

Nancy, with three children in elementary school, works part-time as an
occupational therapist. *"It's hard with three little kids. They want so much.
Any toy they see on TV, they say, 'I want that.' With Christmas coming up you
want to try and get them some of the things they want from on TV. It is like all
your money goes for Christmas and you don't have nothing left for now."*

LaVerne: *"My daughter's birthday is coming up. I haven't got her a thing yet. I
have to pay the dentist one hundred bucks at the end of the month. Her birthday
is coming up right after that and I'm not able to get her anything. So I'm going to
try to borrow some money somewhere. But you can never get ahead, that's the
thing. The worst part about the money situation is you just can't get ahead."*

A Bleak Future for the Children

Carla, twenty-six, is raising three children. *"I think a lot about my oldest
and what her future is going to be like. I want her to have an education. High
school is nothing these days. You have to have more than that. That worries
me. That I have nothing in the bank for her.*

*"She wants to be a teacher. She talks about it all the time. She's a little young
and that might change by the time she graduates. She definitely wants to go to
college. She stays on the honor roll, distinguished honors. She's a real good
student. She's in sixth grade now. I really don't think that I am going to be able
to get a job that will pay all of my bills, for all of us, plus put money in the bank
for her to be able to go to college. I would want all of my three children to go,
but especially her because she's the one that's talking about it.*

*"It's terrible if your child wants an education and you can't do that for
them."*

As these voices reveal, the children hear "no" a lot. And they hear "no" for
things that "all their friends and everyone on TV" seem to have. All parents

hear this lament, regardless of economic circumstances. Yet these mothers can't afford some of the smallest things—new shoes, a night at McDonald's, or a Chicago Bulls cap. These are luxuries.

Single parenting has its stresses and strains. There is no one else to share the fears and bear the responsibilities. But these mothers also live with the overarching worry of money. Will the bills get paid? What if we run out of food? What if something happens? What if I lose this job? What if the rent goes up or my car breaks down? There is no extra money to put away for a child's education. The women struggle just to support their children on a day-to-day basis.

Resourceful Child Raising

Despite their restricted circumstances, many women managed, sometimes very creatively, to find things to do with their children that don't cost much money. Resourceful child raising is what it takes and the women manage to have fun with their children, perhaps putting their money worries on the back burner for a day.

Julie: *"In the winter we have picnics in the living room. We put the sheet on the floor. We make hamburgers. We make potato salad. We have raisins—the whole nine yards. We sit and have a picnic.*

"You learn to do things free. You find out what is free. If there is a reading program that's not too far away and there's enough gas in the car, you go."

Emily: *"On Monday nights we have Brownies for Betty. We have Girl Scouts for Kim on Tuesdays. Wednesday we go to church. I try to do something everyday to get us out of the house. We do the library all the time. Library programs are free. I've searched out all the different free things there are to do."*

Vicki: *"The carnival and the fair are coming up—we will probably go to that. Bowling, miniature golfing, we do that. There is not a whole lot we can do because of the money. We just spend most of our time here at home together, doing homework, reading, or watching TV."*

Amelia: *"My son plays baseball, and we go to all the games here. I've got a Brownie troop this year. If we can, we go to the lake, have a picnic, and stay through lunch and dinner, so they can swim all day. We have a cat and a dog. Wouldn't give them up, either."*

Arlene: *"I try not to sit around and worry about the money because life's too short. I try to have fun. I will take a little bill money every now and then and take the kids to the arcade or to the seventy-five cents movie or just spend a day at the mall. We try to do something and have a little fun because my children and I are not going to miss out on life just because I am in the situation I'm in."*

Renata: *"I had overtime pay for a whole week straight. When I came home that Friday my paycheck was bigger than it had ever been. Me and my kids, we went out. I took them to dinner at Pizza Hut. My son wanted a little pan pizza just for himself, and I bought him that. We had a good time. We caught the bus up and laughed and played on the bus and we caught the bus back. They enjoyed it."*

When Mommy Gets A (Better) Job

Several of the women were in school or in training programs that gave them hope for a better financial future. Their children's reactions to their schooling or jobs were often expressed in terms of having more money.

Connie, who is pursuing a degree in nursing, has two children, ages seven and nine. *"When we go to the store they say, 'Mom, can we have this one day when you get a whole bunch of money?' Or they will say, 'When you are through with college . . . ' That's what their famous line is because I always tell them, 'When I'm through with college . . . ' "*

Susan's five-year-old son is a supporter of her efforts. She is newly certified as a nurse's aide. *"My son is always saying, 'You have to go back to school or you have to do that.' Every once in a while he sees a red sports car and he'll say, 'When you get to be a nurse, you can have that.' "*

Gloria received her associate college degree recently. *"Sometimes my kids say, 'Mom, why can't you buy me this?' or 'Why can't you buy me that?' Now I say, 'Just wait, some day.' "*

These mothers are not different from other parents. They, too, want happy Christmas and holiday mornings and birthdays for their children to remember. Their creativeness and efforts to find fun things to do are ways to make the stone soup tasty.

Dealing with Daddy

The fathers are rarely present in these families. The absence of a father who was abusive or who suffered from alcohol or drug addictions is a help. But the women have been left to deal with the aftermath. The men are gone, but their ghosts are in the psychological scars left on the children.

Even if the children did not experience traumatic incidents, the women must explain the void. "Why did daddy leave?" "Where is daddy?" "Doesn't he love me?" are questions the women handle all the time. To be a family, the women have to explain his absence and abuse in ways that minimize the pain of his loss. "Dealing with daddy" is added to the already difficult work of raising the children alone and in poverty.

Healing the Wounds of Abuse

Amelia's two young children watched as their father beat her up. She describes the effects of this abuse on her children: *"My older child seems okay. 'I've got my mom, that's all I need.' But the abuse hit my younger child much harder. She clams up in this little shell and she won't come out.*

"She drew these pictures of her family life for the counselor she's seeing. Myself and her brother are on one side, on the swings and walking the dog. On the other side she drew her father, in a big, big bucket. 'I don't have a daddy,' she said.

"Yesterday she came home and she did four hours of homework to catch up in school. She will do her work, but she won't pass it in. I asked her why and she said, 'I'm afraid it is not good enough.' Sometimes I don't know what to do. I just hate to see her hurting like that. But the school has been very understanding and the counselor is very helpful."

Gloria's husband abused her and their five children. He raped and molested her daughters. She helped her children heal their personal pain. *"My kids are great. My oldest daughter went through some rough times, but now she is married and has a little girl. My son also went through some pretty rough times. He had a lot of anger from a lot of the things his father put him through and put us through. He's back in school and is thinking about college.*

"My three younger kids have adapted pretty well. Most of the problems they have had has been with their stomach—irritable bowel syndrome and ulcers. It's from all the stress they went through. They all worked with counselors. They were doing poorly in school, but they have brought their grades up. They are much happier kids now.

"They don't talk about their father at all. Two of my children have taken my maiden name, as I did. The three that are home want to change their name. It costs like $250 for each of them to do it and I don't have it. I'm going to try to get it done, one each year at least before they graduate so they can graduate with the 'R' name."

Sally has experienced two tumultuous and abusive marriages. *"My husband walked out when my daughter was five. He had a terrible temper. He*

always made it a point of fighting in front of my daughter when she was a baby.
He wouldn't fight any place else. Finally I told him to leave.

"The second time I was only married a year. I asked him to leave, too. He
was abusive a couple of times to me. But what really broke the straw was when
I found out his son was abusing my daughter. I might have taken it for a while,
but my kid, no. To this day she don't want to talk about it.

"She has a temper that is hard to control. Once we were arguing. She
wanted to leave home. I tried to stop her. She came after me with a butcher
knife. She ended up in the hospital and the whole family went into therapy. She
is doing better now in school and with her temper control."

The children of Amelia, Gloria, and Sally were all involved in very traumatic situations. Amelia, Gloria, and Sally deal with their children's behavioral
and physiological symptoms while relying on a patchwork of counseling help.
At the same time, the women have their own pain to heal as well.

As Amelia stated: *"I've gone through it and I'm trying to help her. Yet I know*
myself that I am still trying to recover from it. I'm still hurting inside. But what I
want most of all is for her hurting to stop. I want her to grow up as a normal
little child. But Mr. Smalley [her counselor] said it is going to take years and
years."

Filling the Void, the Best Way You Know How

Even without severe trauma, the father's absence and abandonment leaves
a void that the mother must try to cope with and explain.

Carol was in an eight-year relationship with her daughter's father. He
walked away from them a few years ago, when the girl was four years old.
Carol describes her little girl's reaction today. *"She clings to me like you would*
not believe. She has this deep-seated fear of abandonment. She has even seen a
psychiatrist about it. When I do anything on my own she asks, 'Mom, are you
trying to get rid of me? Mom, don't you like me?' Trying to convince her all the
time is kind of hard."

Most of the mothers worry about how to explain daddy's absence to their
children. They worry not just about now, but about how their children will
react when they are older.

The father of Anita's little girl hasn't seen her since she was two months old
and has no interest in the child. *"I don't want her to feel demeaned by him in*
any way. I try not to say anything. Now one day when she is older she is going
to ask, you know, questions. She has already asked, 'Where does he live?' I told

her, 'Millerton.' She says, 'Is that far away?' I say, 'No, not really.' She says, 'Well, why doesn't he live with us? Did you get into a fight?' It gets really hard to answer these questions.

"I don't want to bring it up. If she brings it up, fine. One day she will ask where he lives or whatever. If I know, then I'll tell her. It's her decision, not my decision. If she wants to be part of his life and he changes his mind, who knows? Maybe he will be sorry for all that he missed. But I'm not missing out on anything, he is. So if one day she wants to know where he is and I know, then she can go and see him. She can see for herself. She has to make up her own mind."

Connie's ex-husband sees his two children very rarely. "Their father came and took them to the movies twice and they still bring that up. 'What about dad? Can't he take us here or there?' I try to explain why their father doesn't come. I try to be honest. 'Daddy is angry. When daddy gets over being angry, he will come around.' They deal with that. It seems better than lying to them, saying he is away or working."

Susan struggles with the effects of the absent father on her little boy. "I have such mixed feelings about raising him alone. I'm glad that his father and I are divorced. If we would have stayed together, my son would have grew up seeing what his father did. He would have grew up thinking that drinking was cool, that running around was the way to live.

"Now since we live here and my fiancé and I work, he sees what life is about. I anticipate problems with him when he gets to be a teenager because right now he is very confused. His father doesn't come and get him, doesn't see him unless I take him over there. Now he says it's okay that his dad doesn't want to see him, but he is only five. When he's older he's going to have a hard time understanding why.

"So I don't know. I kind of believe in like the Cleaver family. The mom and dad who are so supportive. That's what I wanted to believe when I was younger. When I first had my son I thought, okay, I'll stay home and be the supermom and dad could go out and work. But that's not the way it was. It can't be like that for me anymore.

"I just hope he grows up on the right track. He was too young to remember when we left his dad. Maybe it won't have as much of an impact as I think it will."

LaVerne, never married, is also trying to do the best she can in explaining the absent father and his broken promises to her daughter. "The hardest part about raising my daughter is when she asks about her dad. That's real hard.

When she was little, he never made any contact. He never wrote a letter. He's been in and out of jail.

"She really didn't know she had a dad until his mother came up here to visit her. My daughter didn't even know who she was because they don't send her cards for birthdays or Christmas or nothing like that. His mother said, 'I'm your grandma.' She said, 'No, my grandma lives in Baylerville.' She said, 'I'm your dad's mother' and my daughter said, 'No, I don't have a dad.' I never told her she didn't have a dad. He had just never made contact with her.

"He called her up before school started and said he was going to buy her some clothes. Now she has been calling my mom, asking if her clothes came yet. He told her he was going to send her twenty dollars a month allowance. She hasn't seen it and she has been looking forward to it. So there he is putting things in her head that I got to take back out.

"I try to explain it to her. I sit down and tell her all the problems me and him had and his mental problems. Why I don't want her to see him. Why she is better off where she is at. It might not be better, but it's the best I can do. But at nine, I don't think she understands.

"I told her that when you get to be fifteen or sixteen and want to visit your dad, that's fine. But he will either come here for an hour or you can see him at your grandparents' home for an hour. But you will never leave with him until you are eighteen. My folks say I'm wrong, but they don't know the whole story. They don't know about the drugs and the abuse."

There are no prescribed ways to deal with these situations. The mothers struggle with just how honest to be, especially when abuse or drug or alcohol addiction was involved. They know, as does Susan, that their children are probably better off in a household not disrupted by alcoholic incidents. But they still feel that tug of "but a child needs a father." Perhaps many think, "Yes that's true, but not this one."

They worry that the abandonment will hurt the child's sense of self. But they also worry about protecting their children from a father who may not be responsible enough to be with his children. The residual of the father takes many forms, none of them easy to deal with. To the woman, it can feel like the tail of a dinosaur swatting her just when she thinks she's gotten away.

Some women, themselves raised in a society that promotes the traditional family, are uncomfortable and pained by the loss of what might have been. Eva has two young children and Arlene has three children, the two younger ones of elementary school age.

Eva: *"It's hard, really hard, especially around Christmastime. It really gets to me then that their father is not around to spend time with them. To play like Santa Claus at the door and stuff like that. 'Hurry up and get into bed' . . . like my grandmother used to do to me."*

Arlene: *"It's hard for me being brave about the complete family. It does make a difference. It comes up in school. They are not like the other little kids that have their mom and a dad in the household."*

Women of Hardship

The struggle with financial issues and the worries and insecurities that accompany that struggle are one part of what single parenting in poverty means. Experiencing the pain of not providing for their children is another important aspect. And dealing with the aftereffects of the absent daddy is also in the pot. It is truly a stone soup. Yet the women grapple with all of these and still manage to be a family, and raise their children.

The poverty that these women live with every day can crush the spirit. But most live with a sense of hope that things will get better, a sense of hope inspired by their children. All of the women want their children to grow up and live in better circumstances than they are in now. Some hope that their own positive efforts will be a model for their children.

Not for My Child

Gloria: *"The oldest at home, she wants to go to college. The other one wants to go in the service. My youngest wants to work in radiology. A few years ago all they wanted was to get out of the house. That's all they thought about. But now they think they will live at home and work.*

"I think it was me going back to school because I've noticed they have tried to bring their grades up, too. I tell them, 'If I can do it, you can do it.' Plus I tell them that if they want a nice car or a nice home, you have to have money to do it. You can't make that kind of money working in a restaurant or as a laborer. You have to have an education. They see the job market because I talk to them very honestly about it. They watch what I'm going through. They now understand what life is about."

Renata: *"Working makes me feel important and it makes my kids look up to me. 'My mommy is doing this. She is not at home, doing nothing.' I always tell my daughter, 'If you ever leave me, make sure you have your own money, that*

*you have your own job. You don't have to take no stuff from no man because
you have your own.' I want her to see that in me."*

Jessie: *"I'm going to keep my girls in school. In school they have career days
and people come and show them what they do. Any kind of talent they have, I
want them to develop so they have a choice. I'm definitely letting them know
that life is not a fairy tale. You don't get married and stay home, and live
happily ever after."*

Pat: *"I want so badly for them to not make the mistakes I did. I want them to
go to college. I want them to be productive in their life. I want them to be happy
over all, no matter what happens. I guess that's what every parent wants for
their children."*

The pain of not providing for their children is close to the surface for most
of the women. Yet, at the same time, the effort to provide and be a family is
what keeps them going. If it means going to the Food Basket or leaning on
local charities for food and clothes, then they do it. These women worry about
the price of gum, say "no" to a child's wish for a movie or new dress, feel
miserable when they can't buy a school book, and try to have fun doing free
things with their children. They juggle exhausting schedules of work, school,
and child rearing so that they can get better jobs and improve their lives. They
deal with the scars on their children left by the dad and explain his absence in
the best way that they can. There is little time or opportunity to heal their own
pain and loss. They work to overcome hardships, forging a life within circumscribed situations.

SIX. **Working**

Hitting the Cellar Ceiling

What kinds of work do the women do? What jobs have they held? How do they experience these jobs? Most of the women have held a variety of jobs, usually minimum wage or low-paying ones, since the age of sixteen or seventeen. Their work histories usually begin with "I have always worked," and end with "I really like working." The jobs mentioned most frequently fall into three major categories: factory work, waitressing, and caregiving. The women work hard for the money in the factories, see waitressing as their best hope for job flexibility, and genuinely like the caregiving jobs, especially the ability to help others. In describing their work experiences—what they do, and what they like and dislike about their jobs—the women present a detailed picture of their work lives.

Factory Work: She Works Hard for the Money

More than half of the women have worked in one or more factory jobs. They have helped produce cartons, cookies, lightbulbs, dog bones, sneakers, and turkey parts.

Too Many Rules

Jean, the mother of five children, completed her GED after leaving her abusive husband and now works in a food-processing plant. *"I work in Ruttle Food Company. I tray pack. What you do is trim the meat, the drumsticks or whatever, put them on trays, package them up, and box them. I really don't mind the job. We do different things—anywhere from trimming the meat to packing it up. It is not one dull boring job the whole day long. You are jumping around from one thing to another and it's interesting. The people I work with are great. They are fun to get along with. We carry on. It makes the day go faster. It's like a family.*

"I just had a performance evaluation by the lead person and she is pleased with my job performance. I'm going to do something else now, clipping wings. Right now I'm getting $6.05 an hour. I started out at $5.80 an hour. After thirty days you get a quarter raise and after sixty days another quarter raise.

"I don't like my supervisor. He can't look you in the eye and say 'hi' to you. Even if you say hello to him, he won't look you in the eye. The only time he talks to you is if he has a problem with you.

"All the rules really get to me. During the first sixty days, your probationary period, you are not allowed to miss two days. Well, I missed two days. My car broke down. I couldn't find one over the weekend, so I had to take Monday off to get a car. Then I missed another day and left work ten minutes early one day because I was sick. Now they have extended my probationary period. They say if I miss one more day, come in late, or leave early during the next month, you're terminated and they will do it.

"Last Tuesday I made it by a hair. My car was being worked on again and my brother's girlfriend forgot to pick me up. I got there two minutes before seven. A girl who started with me was five minutes late, and she was fired. But if I get a phone call and one of my kids is sick, you better believe I'm out of here. Let them fire me, that's ridiculous. Kids get contagiously sick and you cannot take them to child care."

A Tough Dirty Job

Marilyn is the mother of two teenagers and a young boy with medical problems. She left school after completing the tenth grade and has worked in a variety of jobs ever since. *"I worked for four years in a foundry. They made anything from cast-iron doorstops to manhole covers. It's good money. I made $8.45 an hour and I went from $7.02 to $8.45 in three months. That's good money. Normally I would work from three in the afternoon until midnight. But sometimes you had to work a lot more. It is nonunion so you have to do it. Many times we worked from one in the afternoon until three in the morning. And that was six days a week.*

"I worked on the sorting line. You have to break castings off of the molds. Like, if it's a barbell, we made barbells, you pick the weight up, slam it on the side of the line to break the mold casting off. You take an air gun, sort of like a dentist's drill with a sander on it, and sand the barbell down smooth. Then you take it over and slide it down a chute. I would do like three or four of these a minute. The work can be hard, lifting all night. I got tendinitis in both of my arms.

"There are about five people on a sorting line. It's very noisy and very dirty. You have to take a shower before you leave there. It's black sand and oil, pieces of cast-iron metal. You get it in your hair. You are all black. You look like you came out of the coal mine.

"They really don't train you. You just put your ear cuffs on, you wear your safety glasses and steel-tip shoes, and go down the stairs. I had a super boss. His boss would come out and yell at him. Then he would come over and say 'Hey, look, you did this wrong but I am supposed to really yell at you, so bear with me.' Then he would scream at the top of lungs at you, so the big guys would understand that he was yelling at you. Then he would say, 'I'm sorry I had to do that.'

"You get two fifteen-minute breaks and thirty-five minutes for lunch. They shut down two weeks in the summer. Once you've been there a year, you get paid one week, and the other you don't get paid. After five years you get a whole whopping two weeks. That's still during the shutdown weeks.

"I don't know if I could have gone any further. You work there. That's it. That's as far as you go. After five or six months you might get a quarter raise. But I started to get more raises, almost up to $2.80 through my work. I probably would have worked my way up, probably to the weighing scale. They

bring the parts over, you weigh them, and that's how they can determine how many parts are in or how many parts are missing."

Working on the Line

Renata, the mother of two teenagers, has held a variety of factory jobs. *"I worked on the assembly line at the lighting company for six years. We made lightbulbs. These long lights would come down the line. They would be open and we would have to put the ballast in. The ballast is like a big battery. It goes in first and then we would have to wire the batteries to where the lightbulbs would hook in. The lights would go on down the line and somebody would put the cover over the battery and at the end someone would put the glass over it.*

"I learned how to do each one of the jobs so if someone didn't come in or there was a new person, I would do the most important job. I was most proud of learning how to ballast because that was the fastest position there. You really didn't have time to think when the lights started coming down the line. I lost a lot of weight. I was mostly twisting all day long. It was great exercise.

"I felt good on that job. I knew what I was doing and I could explain it to someone else. I could show it to someone else. I never had a problem. I made $6.35 an hour. We had good benefits—hospitalization, dental, all of that.

"I made supervisor a couple of times. When the supervisor for our belt didn't come in, I would supervise. I get along very well with people. I liked being the supervisor. If the supervisor didn't come in, I would go to the supervisor over me and tell him that I needed someone to take my spot, while I took the supervisor's spot.

"There wasn't any opportunity for me to be a permanent supervisor. The place was full. If someone didn't come in, then I was on the list to take that position for that day. But to be permanent, someone would have to quit and then I would have to move up a ladder. It would make me one more step closer to being a permanent supervisor, but they always had enough supervisors. Nobody quit. If I had been a supervisor I wouldn't have had to stand on my feet as much. Working on the line, I had to stand on my feet all day, every day, for six years."

LaVerne, never married, a high school graduate and the mother of one child, has worked in restaurants, factories, and construction. *"I worked at a dog-bone factory. They would bring in big sheets of rawhide. Then they would rinse them off because they have bleach and stuff on them. Then they would give you some little squares and we had to roll them up and tie knots in them.*

"My boss was okay, but I didn't like the girls on the line. It was minimum wage and piece rate. The girls were really nasty. You are standing beside someone and they are bitching because you have a little bit more work than they did. I don't enjoy that. We are all there for the same purpose, to work."

Vicki is divorced and the mother of two children. *"The worst job I ever had was in a cookie factory. It was an assembly line. The cookies came down the line and you had to be super fast. These older women had been there for years and they could do it. It was terrible. You just had cookies flying everywhere. I was up to my knees in cookies. It was animal cookies. I won't forget that."*

Life in the Sewing Factories

LaVerne: *"I worked at the coat sewing factory for almost two years. Everything had to be perfect, not a stitch could be out of place. The small parts had to be perfect too. I had to outline a small part and it would go on to the next lady. She could tell if you made a stitch out and then they would bring it back. It was really nerve-racking. You weren't allowed to talk to the people who sat beside you. And you were sitting pretty close to them. The ladies would cry if you got more work than they got. Then they would end up arguing. It was crazy.*

"It was a forty-hour-a-week job and then I worked half-time on Saturday. It was a good-paying job. I made pretty good money. It started out minimum wage, but it was piece rate. If you sat there all day long, except for your half-hour break, you'd make seven or eight dollars an hour.

"I think most of the same people are still there. I guess it's the money. Constantly they just sit there all day long. They don't even get up and go to the bathroom. They get up and eat their lunch, and that's it. It was mostly women that did the sewing. They had bundle boys that bring you the work."

Sally, a high school graduate, is divorced with two children. *"I worked in a shoe factory. I liked it. I worked there for two years, sewing shoes. That may sound nuts, because a lot of people say factory work is nerve-racking. But I was making pretty good money. I was on piece rate. The factory pay was about three dollars an hour. There was times when I was making six or seven dollars an hour.*

"The job was fine, but the people got to me. Many of the older women were set in their ways. There was a lot of people who were jealous because of how

good I was and how fast I was. They started a bunch of stuff and made it unpleasant for me."

Jessie is divorced and has two elementary-school-age children living at home. *"I worked for a while in a shoe company. I would sit at the sewing machine. The material would be lined up and I would sew tongues on tennis shoes all day. You would work for two hours, get a fifteen-minute break, then work for two hours, have lunch, then two more hours of work, another break, two more hours of work and go home."*

Factory Work: Close-up

The women do, indeed, work hard for the money. Yet, for the most part, they do not complain about the work itself. Although the job might be tedious, dirty, or unpleasant, they prefer longer, rather than shorter hours. Their reason for liking the job is the money. "It was a good-paying job," so the work was okay. Those working on piece rate are able to earn above minimum wage by working fast and taking few breaks during the day.

The women distinguished an okay job from a poor one by how they were treated by the people around them. Getting along with co-workers and bosses could make these jobs tolerable and even pleasant. But unfriendly bosses and co-workers contribute to job dissatisfaction.

Waitressing: Flexibility, but No Future

Many of the women move back and forth between factory jobs and waitressing. Of the two, waitressing is usually the preferred job. More than three-fourths of the women have worked as a waitress at some point in their lives. The major reasons for liking the job are the "tips and customers." It is also often described as "fun."

Sheila, a high school graduate, is separated and the mother of three children. *"I worked in a supper club as a barmaid. I was making good money though I had to work late hours. You would go in at five and leave at two in the morning, six days a week. I had this job for quite a while. It was fun. I liked it. If the people like you, you would get nice tips, especially Thursdays and Fridays."*

Jessie: *"I like working in a restaurant. It's different. It's not like a factory job where you do the same thing every day. You get to talk to people. I like working with people basically and I like the money every day, the tips. You get used to bringing home a little bit of cash every day. It's hard when you go to a job where you have to wait two weeks to get paid."*

In addition to the people and the money, there are other reasons for choosing waitressing. For some it is very much "what I do" and, as such, a form of job security. For others, it is a way to earn a reasonable amount of money and still have an acceptable work and family balance.

It's What I Do

Judy and Anita, who started waitressing as teenagers, have never held any other type of job.

Judy, twenty-nine, has two young children and did not complete high school. *"I've only had one job, as a waitress. I quit school at sixteen and went to work for the Como Place Restaurant. I worked there for six years. Me, mom, and my two older sisters all worked there. We just ran the place like it was ours. Then I only worked for Fiatel Restaurant for four years. Because I only worked for the Como Place Restaurant, Fiatel Restaurant hired me over the telephone. I'm going back to Fiatel Restaurant in January. I can go back anytime I want to. People ask how many jobs I've had, I say one.*

"It's hard, but basically it's fine. You meet a lot of customers, different people, and you get to know them. I like the waitress work. It's fun waitressing and waiting on people. When I go back I'll make about $40 a day in tips. As I get to know the people, it will get higher. My actual wage is $2.09 an hour. I rely on that for my medical benefits. They take out $32 per week for Blue Cross–Blue Shield."

Anita, twenty-six, completed high school and has one young child. *"I waitress. I have always waitressed. I have been a waitress since I was sixteen. I like the job. I like associating with people. I am with different people all the time. I enjoy talking to them and waiting on them. I couldn't stand being in a factory, standing in one position, doing the same thing every day. Sure I serve food every day, but the people are different every day. You learn a lot.*

"I have worked in three restaurants. I worked at the Hot Spot for three years. I started there when I was sixteen. Then I went to Don's for about five years. I liked it there but the hours didn't work for me after my daughter was born. So I went to Ream's. I told them the hours I wanted and it has worked out. I've been there close to three years.

"They didn't want me to quit at Don's. But I couldn't take those hours. So I quit and Ream's hired me the next day. Waitress jobs are a dime a dozen. It may be minimum wage, but it's work.

"I really enjoy working with people. I just feel good about myself, knowing I did a good job, especially when I count my money in my pocket. I make good money. If I could work seven days a week, like some of the girls who don't have kids do, I could do very well."

Balancing Work and Family

As discussed in chapter 4, many of the women see waitressing as a way to earn a reasonable income, while still having time to spend with their children.

Anita's daughter is five years old. *"I work three days a week. I work 5 PM to 10 PM on Thursday, 2 PM to 10 PM on Saturday and Sunday and the rest of the time I spend with my daughter. So it works out well.*

"I make $2.35 an hour, plus my tips. I usually make about $200 to $250 a week. The only reason I don't work full-time is that she needs to know I am here because he [her daughter's father] isn't here. She needs to know she has me to depend on."

Meg, twenty-one, is a high school graduate and has an infant daughter. *"I'm a waitress and I work about twenty-five hours a week. But I make decent money, so that's all I have to work. The baby's father also pays twenty-five dollars a week for child support. I just receive a medical card. I've never received cash assistance, or anything like that.*

"I make about two hundred dollars a week, which isn't bad for twenty-five hours. My aunt and everyone say, 'Why don't you find a better job, one with benefits and all that?' Well, when she is little like this I'd rather work twenty-five hours and get that amount of money, than work more and not spend time with her. That, to me, is more important.

"I like the people, the customers. You meet so many people being a waitress. There are some things about the job that aren't so great, but the people make it worth it. There's not too much supervision. If customers ask to sit in your section, then you know they like you."

Bobbie, thirty-two, did not finish high school and has an eleven-year-old son and an infant daughter. *"I work Saturdays, 6:30 in the morning until 6:30 at night and Sundays, 11 AM to 6 PM, tending bar. On Mondays I work 11:30 AM to 1 PM in the kitchen to help out over lunch. I like working with the people. I make great tips.*

"I bring home about $200 to $225 for those days. That ain't bad. And I have my whole week off with the kids. I'm not with them much on the weekends, because of work. Saturdays are really bad because that's twelve hours. But on

Sundays we get up and have a big breakfast together, me and my son. We don't have no time on the weekends, which I don't like.

"The bartending job I have is great. When I'm there, I'm in charge of the restaurant. What I say goes. That's what I like, mainly. On Saturdays I work the whole restaurant by myself. I wait on the coffee shop on the side, the bar, the dining room. Breakfast is packed, but that's okay. I can handle that. I'd rather work the whole day by myself. Everyone that comes in on the weekends knows it's me. If they have to wait a couple of minutes, they know it's for a good reason."

Evaluating the Waitressing Job

In the United States, waitressing jobs have always been "women's work." For unskilled women with limited employment opportunities, it has many positive aspects. First, interacting with different people is an asset: it's what makes the job "fun." Second, the job, because of the tips, pays fairly well. Third, the tipping system provides direct feedback and a sense of control over outcomes. The more hours waitresses work, the more tips they get. The better they interact with the customers, the more tips they get. Furthermore, the tipping system is a way to get paid every day. This provides direct rewards, as well as much needed money on the spot.

Fourth, the flexible hours and the variations in scheduling opportunities are also important positive features. They can schedule work hours and workdays so as to spend more time with their children, especially with the young children. The job gives them some control in balancing work and family. Fifth, these jobs can also provide some sense of work autonomy. Although the job duties are fairly prescribed, there is no boss looking over a waitress's shoulder every minute. In some jobs the waitresses work alone or with one other waitress. Finally, the job provides a sense of employment security, because jobs are always available. As Anita said, "Waitress jobs are a dime a dozen."

These positive features, however, might also be put into the pot of stone soup—making something out of nothing. When compared to the alternative of factory work, waitressing seems to have more attractive features. It has a more direct and positive reward and feedback system, more opportunity to be with a variety of people, less rigid supervision, and greater flexibility of hours and scheduling than does factory work. But within the context of jobs in general, both choices would be rated low in comparison to other employment opportunities. Lacking education and training, however, the women have few job options.

Forced to choose between a factory and a waitressing job, the latter may be the better alternative. But neither job, especially waitressing, is a good long-term solution for a woman raising children alone. The part-time restaurant jobs offer no benefits. There are no health or dental benefits, life insurance, or retirement programs. The price the women pay in the long run for some semblance of control is a big one. Moreover, there are no advancement opportunities. After working ten years as waitresses, Judy and Anita are still doing the same job. And if they continue another ten years, they will still be doing the same job. Lastly, the late shifts and the concentrated hours can be helpful when children are young. But when the children enter their teenage years, the evening and weekend work schedules that produce the most income are the same times that the mother needs to be at home or watchful of her children's activities. As a short-run solution, it is not unreasonable. As a long-term occupation, it has many pitfalls.

Caregiving: Helping Others

Caregiving differs from the other two categories of jobs in that it is the only one in which the women expressed a strong liking for the job itself. The appeal of the factory job is money and that of the waitressing job is flexibility. For those in the caregiving jobs, such as nursing aides, it is what their work means to others and their ability to help others through the job that is most attractive. There are fewer women pursuing jobs in this area, mainly because it requires some prior training. Several women who were working in other types of jobs said that they had always wanted to be a nurse.

Nancy, twenty-five, works part-time as an occupational therapist's aide and is pursuing an associate degree part-time in the same field. She has three young children. *"I only work part-time now. I work from 9 AM until 1:30 PM every day. My job is only supposed to be getting the patients from their rooms, taking them to the therapist's room, and bringing them back. But I do just about everything there. I do all the copying. I file the reports. I'm more or less like a girl Friday.*

"What I like best is working with the people. They are really fun. I like working with older people. When I graduate I want to work with geriatric people. I really like talking to the patients. There are so many things you can learn from them. They like to talk about when they were younger. Everybody's

life is different. This one man tells us the same thing over and over again. But you never get tired of hearing him.

"I make $5.10 an hour. We get paid every two weeks. That is one of the things I don't like about the job. I would rather be paid weekly than every two weeks."

Susan, twenty-two, the mother of a young boy, has just become certified as a nurse's aide. *"I've always wanted to be a nurse. I just really like what nurses do and I like caring for people. I would like to be an LPN eventually. Nurse's aide is a first step.*

"I've had three weeks of nurse's aide training. I've put in to train in the Alzheimer's unit. Even if I don't get to work with them, I'll know how to deal with the confused patients.

"I've been doing this for six months and just passed my certification exam last month. I work almost full-time. When I'm guaranteed ten full days for two weeks, it will be full-time. I work from three in the afternoon until eleven at night. It pays $5.70 an hour. I get paid every two weeks and it's about $300. It will be a little more when I'm full-time, plus I will have medical, dental, and vacation pay.

"Basically the job is to give care to the residents of the nursing home. We wash them, we feed them, we take them to the bathroom. You have to lift them out of bed, into their wheelchairs.

"We help out the LPNs, like we're their right hand, really. There was a new guy in, he had above-the-knee amputations. He was supposed to stay in bed. He was restrained. Somehow, he tried to climb out and hit his head. There was blood gushing everywhere. When I checked his room, I found him. I didn't touch him. I ran out and got all the LPNs that I could find. Everyone told me that I did a good job, that anyone else would have panicked and tried to put him back in bed. I knew better than to touch him. That night I came home and really felt good because I knew what I was doing at that point.

"I'm still afraid of the death and dying part. I don't want to get attached to people and find out they have died. I've only helped once, we have to wash and wrap them, and I took it pretty well.

"My two supervisors, they are really down to earth. If I make a mistake, they don't jump on you. They are pretty nice. I get along with them. I get along with everybody I work with.

"I'm most proud of the fact that I'm actually doing something for all these people who can't do something for themselves. Last night there were two ladies in the hallway. One was in the wheelchair and wanted to go to bed. Another lady passed her and said, 'Ask Susan to put you to bed. I know she will, she's a

nice girl.' She didn't realize I was standing there. That's the proudest thing to me, to know that they know they can count on me if they need help. That's what is really fulfilling about the whole thing.

"I think I want to start going to school to be an LPN. I would like to be the med nurse who passes the meds around all night. The vo-tech has a program here. It is a year course. I'm kind of tossing it in my mind. Do I want to stop as an LPN or do I want to go another year to be an RN? I think if I was guaranteed a medical nurse position, I would be satisfied with that."

Since her divorce nine years ago, Vicki, thirty, has held a variety of jobs to support herself and her two children. She worked for the last five years in a nursing home. *"I loved that job. The people, the older people, you grow so close with them. It is like seeing your grandma and grandpa again. I just love them to death. I miss that part of the job.*

"I was in housekeeping and I also was a nurse's aide. I did both. I was in housekeeping during the daytime and I worked second shift then for the nursing assistant. Generally I worked 7 AM to 2 PM for housekeeping and 3 PM until 9 PM on the second shift. But every day the hours were different.

"I went to school at the home for six months to be trained. You feed the patients, change the patients, bathe them, read to them, and transport them back and forth to the activity room or to therapy. In housekeeping, you would clean the patients' rooms.

"When I started I earned $5.25. When I left I was earning $7.75 an hour. Sometimes we would work overtime. Sometimes I would bring home $250 to $260 a week, something like that.

"I never missed any work. They really liked my performance. My boss, she gave me a really good evaluation. I'm most proud of how I helped people there. When they would be crying or upset, I would go in and talk to them. You really grow close to them. I still go visit them. At Christmastime I take my children up there and we sing carols with them."

Rating the Caregiving Job

If the women had been asked, they probably would have rated these jobs as higher than either factory work or waitressing on performance feedback, advancement, people, quality of supervision, working conditions, and benefits. Also, if they are able to continue schooling, there are opportunities to advance, such as to be an occupational therapist, LPN, or RN. But the selling point for these women is the job itself, the ability to help others.

Some Odd Jobs

A host of other jobs were mentioned, but no clear category emerged. Other jobs held included: art teacher, furniture refinisher, file clerk, telemarketer, office maintenance, paralegal, barber, and auto transporter. Only one woman ever held secretarial jobs and with two exceptions, nontraditional, primarily male-dominated jobs were not mentioned.

File Clerk

Marie, thirty-one, a high school graduate and the mother of three children, has held a civil service clerical job for seven years. *"I'm a file clerk and in the process of becoming an applications clerk. As a file clerk I make labels, pull folders, replace them. I like processing the applications. I'm really learning what the agency is all about.*

"I work with one other woman, in a unit of about twenty people. I really like my boss. Each year I have been getting an increase. After three years I was making $6.00 or $6.50 an hour. Now I make $8.33 an hour. If I am upgraded to a GS 5 it will be $9.07 an hour."

Office Maintenance

Carla, twenty-six, has three children and did not complete high school. *"For five or six years I worked in an office building and cleaned the rooms. I did odd jobs for the owners, but my main job was cleaning. I cleaned from 9 AM to 6 PM every day. When I left there I was making five dollars an hour. When I first started there I thought I would work there for a while and then find something else, but it didn't happen that way, so I just stayed. It kept me busy. The time went so quick because you were busy all day. I know it sounds crazy, but I like to clean. But I didn't like the pay and there was no opportunity to go anywhere."*

Auto Transporter

Nontraditional jobs were extremely unusual. Eva, twenty-two, has two young children and did not complete high school. She was a car transporter for four years. *"I transported cars from state to state. When I first started I was making $3.75 an hour. When I left I was making $5.25. That's because we didn't have a union or anything. Usually I would work sixteen hours a day, about three days a week. The parts I liked best were the traveling, meeting new people, and being by myself. The part I liked least was working with the old* *men. It's mainly a man's job. I got hassled a lot, they're fresh. I just ignored it. Most of the men were very nice, but some were perverts. There were a handful of women, but they were old too. I was the youngest person there.*

"My boss was all right. He was a shuttler too, but he forgot about how it was back then and never really tried to help anybody. I wanted to become a rental agent. They send you to school and everything. But he was no help. I would ask him but all he kept saying was, 'I'll try.' But nothing happened. I wanted to be a rental agent to get some benefits. I had no medical coverage. Every time I took my son to the doctor, I had to pay for it.

"I am proud, though, for having the job and being in it so long. I finally quit because I got hurt in an accident with the van and they wouldn't help me out with my medical bills and stuff."

Looking at the Odd Jobs

The cleaning job and the auto transporter jobs share some of the characteristics of factory and waitressing jobs. Specifically, these are jobs the women "can get." They require no prior training or skills. The auto transporter job, similar to waitressing, has the short-run advantage of flexibility of hours and some interesting features, such as traveling and meeting people. But, like waitressing, it has no benefits and few advancement opportunities.

Marie seems to have the best job. It has benefits, security, advancement (albeit slow), good supervision, performance feedback, and reasonable working conditions. Like the advancement, the money is fairly good, but slow in coming. Her office job did not seem to have any intrinsic excitement, although the possibility of learning something new was present. Ironically, Marie is one of the women who really wants to be a nurse. But she doesn't see how she could go back to school full-time and support her three children. She concluded, *"I see myself still here at Farrow Company. I know as the years go by my salary will increase and someday I will be okay."*

Job Vulnerability

The kinds of jobs the women qualify for tend to be those that do not provide assistance or flexibility if they experience child care or personal health problems. The women lack the influence to request changes or temporary solutions to their problems within the work system. They are voiceless and vulnerable. For several women, a job loss due to child care or personal health problems forced them onto public assistance.

Child Care–Work Conflicts

LaVerne, Julie, and Jean all experienced child care–work conflicts, but they were not in jobs that would accommodate their needs. Their jobs offered no flexibility and the women either had to do as they were told, quit, or be fired.

Julie would not bring her children out in the cold winter weather, nor could she get a baby-sitter at night. She was forced to quit her job at the supermarket and had to seek public assistance in order to care for her family. LaVerne, working in a dog-bone factory, missed a lot of work because her child was sick. She was fired and had to go on public assistance.

Jean had her starting time switched from 7 AM to 6 AM. This new schedule posed child-care problems for her, as the day-care center did not open until 6:30 AM. The food-processing plant, which employed a lot of single mothers, ignored the negative impact of the rescheduling on its employees. Rather, it placed the burden on the women to either reschedule or, as Jean is trying to do, get another job. In the meantime, Jean and her children must now start their day at 4:30 AM to accommodate her employer.

In all three situations, the employers expected commitment and loyalty and were quick to punish the women when it was lacking. But the employers displayed no commitment to the women in return. They were not willing to be flexible or consider short-term accommodations to personal circumstances.

Health Problems

Three women described situations in which health problems caused them to leave their jobs.

Sally: *"I worked in a restaurant for over two years. Then a new manager came in and I was fired. I had health problems and the new boss really didn't like that. I had varicose veins, mainly from the long hours of standing. I tried to see about unemployment. I had to fight to get that. She didn't want to pay a red cent to anybody. I fought for it and finally got it.*

"Now it's hard to get another job and my health is getting worse. I love working and I'd rather be busy at work and making my own money. But I'm not going to risk losing my leg over it. My health is more important."

Renata: *"I had to leave the lighting factory because I had rheumatoid arthritis in both ankles. It was very painful and had gotten to the point that I could barely walk. At the doctor's suggestion, I stayed home for a while, but it didn't get any better.*

"He said I would have to quit my job. 'Is there anything else you could do where you could sit down and work?' I said 'No, I work on the assembly line and that's a majority of the time standing up.' I didn't want to quit. I just wanted to take a long leave of absence and get better. But to get public assistance, I had to quit. Without that job, I had no way to support my family."

Vicki: "I worked in the nursing home five years. Then they started using a new cleaning chemical. The whole year it bothered me. I started getting sick a lot and started missing work because I was sick. It was more or less poisoning my body. I still have scars on my wrists from it. The doctor said I can't be around that chemical. But the nursing home had no other work for me to do because I would be around that chemical and it had to be used. I was very sick and the doctor said if I stayed there I would end up in the hospital. I had no other choice but to quit.

"I tried to get workman's compensation, but it didn't go through. They denied it and I lost the appeal. I had no choice but to go on public assistance. It's really hard. I love working in nursing homes, but most of them use that chemical. Now I'm trying to find work in a factory, assembly line places, but I miss the nursing home and the people."

Ironically, the women's health problems are both job-related and job-threatening. Sally has held jobs only in factories and restaurants, and both pose dangers to her health now. Renata is advised not to return to any assembly line work, her only prior work experience. Similarly, Vicki's allergic reaction precludes her from working in the area she loves, in nursing homes with older people. Their health problems stem from doing the only kinds of jobs available to them and their limited job skills make it difficult to find work that won't aggravate their health problems.

The Meaning of Work

The meaning of work differs among the women. For many it is related directly to money. For others, work means personal control and responsibility. And to others it is related to image and self-esteem.

The responses relating work to money are very clear.

Eva: "Work means the money, the money. Once I was working two jobs, but it was breaking my health."

Judy: "To make your bills and payments—you got to work to make your payments."

Work as a means of enhancing personal control and responsibility is illustrated by the following:

Vicki: *"It means you have responsibility. I like working. I feel confident in working, in making my own money and supporting myself and my children."*

Susan: *"Well, it means two things to me. First, I can count on a paycheck. If my son needs something, I don't have to sit around and wait for a welfare check. Now I can count on going in every other Monday and knowing that I have twice as much as I made on welfare. It means a lot.*

"It also means a lot to me that I can go in there and I'm able to do for these people what they can't do themselves. There is really two sides of it. I'm taking care of my family on the one hand, but yet I'm taking care of somebody else's grandmother on the other."

Joy: *"It means going out there and earning a living—making a living for yourself."*

LaVerne: *"Working means a pay check. It means getting up and going out and doing it. It makes me feel good that I can get up and go do it. I've always been a worker. I used to work in restaurants when I was fourteen, and baby-sat ever since I was nine. I always had money in my pocket and if I wanted something I would work for it and buy it myself."*

And for some women the meaning of work is related to self-image.

Renata: *"Working makes me feel important and it makes my kids look up to me."*

Hitting the Cellar Ceiling

What emerges from all of the work stories is a picture of the women as marginalized from the working mainstream, as vulnerable and powerless in low-paying jobs. They have limited knowledge of the range of job opportunities available, but they express a positive attitude toward working. They occupy jobs in the basement, working hard only to hit their heads on the "cellar ceiling."

In the Cellar

The majority of the jobs previously or presently held by most of the women are leading nowhere. They are out of the mainstream of occupations or organizations that provide advancement or opportunities for further training. The piece-rate worker or the waitress can work hard and earn a little bit more money by these efforts. But their efforts will not lead to a better job. There are no avenues of opportunity characteristic of career-oriented jobs. There is no organization to spot talent, provide training, or develop potential. Their job experiences are isolated, with little or no opportunity to build a future. For these women, starting at the bottom means staying at the bottom.

Replaceable

The women are rarely in systems—organizations or occupations—that feel any sense of responsibility to them as employees. Factory piece-rate workers are easily replaced. Any family emergency, such as a sick child, or a health problem, such as swollen legs or hands, means an exit for the employee and a new worker is hired in her place. The worker bends to the job rules or leaves. The employer feels no obligation to find a temporary job for the women with a health problem or provide any scheduling flexibility so that the sick child can receive medical attention. Ironically, the women who need organizational help the most are often in marginalized job situations that lack supportive employee benefits.

Women's Work—Women's Wages

Most of the jobs are those traditionally held by women. As with most "women's work," they are low-paying jobs. The factory women spoke of $7.00 an hour as good money. That's $14,560 annually. The waitresses were proud of roughly $300 a week or $15,600, without any benefits. The nurse's aides jobs were in the range of $5.50 to $7.75 an hour, or $11,440 to $16,120 per year. These are not the annual wages of secondary wage earners, women dependent on men who are the family breadwinners. These women *are* the breadwinners whose annual salaries must support a family of three or four. Working full-time, a woman with three children might earn $14,560 per year. If she does, she is still below the 1993 U.S. poverty threshold of $14,705 for a family of four. Working full-time, the women and her family are just scraping by.

The expansion of the earned-income tax credit (EITC) in the Omnibus Budget Reconciliation Act of 1993 (OBRA93) will help low-income households. By 1996, the working poor will be eligible for up to $3,370 in tax credits. In effect, the EITC can raise an hourly wage of $4.25 to $5.70 or $5.95 (see Haveman and Scholz 1994). While it will certainly help to make work pay (Bane and Ellwood 1994), it cannot turn a low-wage job into a high-wage one or one with opportunities for significant income growth. The women can expect little change in their incomes over the next ten or so years, years when the financial needs of their children will increase. Emergencies will occur that may deplete whatever savings they have. The marginalized nature of their work experiences, the susceptibility to job loss, and the low-wage jobs point to a bleak working future for these women. Over the years, after forty hours a week at a sewing machine or late nights pouring coffee in the restaurant, they will look up from these basement jobs and feel the pain as their heads hit the cellar ceiling.

Limited Knowledge of Occupations

Discussions about work revealed that most of the women had limited knowledge about the range of occupations or jobs that might be available to them. Restaurant work or factory work were jobs they knew about or had heard about from friends and family. Even women attempting some job or occupational choice spoke of very traditional, female-dominated jobs. Many women wanted to pursue a career as a beautician. Nursing was the most frequently mentioned occupation of choice, often seen as a "dream job."

Even their range of knowledge of opportunities within traditional jobs was limited. Nursing was well known, but other jobs within the caregiving field were not. Nancy, pursuing a future as an occupational therapist, said she had never heard of this position until she met the woman who became her boss. Office jobs were not commonly held. If anything, the women spoke of office jobs as something they might train for, as jobs for the future.

Like Mother, Like Daughter

A restricted range of aspirations and limited knowledge of occupations and jobs available was true of their mothers as well. Most of their mothers did not work outside of the home and many raised large families. But the few mothers who were employed occupied the same limited range of jobs—waitress, cook, beautician, factory worker, and nurse's aide. Their daughters followed suit. Renata, who worked in the lighting factory, had a mother who spent her whole working life in a coat factory.

Renata describes her mother's efforts with great pride. *"My mother worked in the C&T coat factory. I worked there too for a while. I used to tease her and say 'Hey, mom, if you close your eyes you could find your way there anyway.' Rain, snow, hail, or sleet, she would go to work. Sometimes I would feel so bad.*

'Mom, it is raining so hard, or there is so much snow, do you have to go to work?' and she would say, 'Who is going to take care of you if I don't go to work?' "

Three women who were waitresses or who had worked in restaurants had mothers who did the same thing. Sally noted, *"My mother worked in a restaurant. She still does today. She said, 'If you want to stay hired, stay in a restaurant.'"* And Bobbie said, *"My mother was this county's best waitress, she said."*

Connie is in school pursuing a nursing degree. She, too, spoke proudly of her mother. *"My mom was a cook when I was growing up, but now she is a nursing assistant. She went back to school. I drove her. She does all private duty with the elderly. My father complained. He didn't want her to go to school."*

On the positive side is the warmth and pride expressed in describing a mother's efforts. But on the negative, we hear a replay of the same "going nowhere" jobs not unusual for women. The restrictions imposed on the mothers as women not expected to have careers or as women blocked from other jobs or occupations, are again experienced by their daughters. They, too, now occupy the jobs in the basement, working hard, but going no further than the cellar ceiling.

Positive Attitude, but Bleak Outlook

What emerges is a generally positive attitude toward both the jobs the women do and working in general. While some of the factory workers expressed dissatisfactions with aspects of their jobs, most still had a positive view of the jobs in general. Jean liked her work and Sally said she liked the sewing machine factory job. The waitresses say the work is "fun" and "enjoyable." Those in other jobs said "I love my job." Working means money, more control over their lives, and a positive self-image. The women work hard at jobs that have many undesirable aspects, yet they are able to maintain a positive attitude toward work and working.

The women's past and present job scenarios are bleak. Lacking the requisite education and training, their options are few. The devaluation of and low wages attached to women's work and the strong cultural forces that channel women into these jobs pose more problems than promise for their employment futures.

The impact on poor single mothers of working in the margins is reflected in LaVerne's comments. *"I don't know why life should be so hard. Life seems like*

I get on a boat and I get going and something happens and then I fall back again. Then I have to start all over again. Then I get back in the boat and work hard and then something happens and I have to start all over again. It seems like I never get anywhere but I work real hard. The big question for me would be to figure out how I could get somewhere and stay there and keep going. But I don't know how to do that."

SEVEN. What Helps?

The Role of Social Support

These women face many difficult circumstances: poverty, relationship losses, the aftereffects of living with an abuser or addicted mate, balancing work and family, returning to school, and raising children alone. What helps? What makes it all a little easier? What has made some of their positive efforts possible? Social support plays an important role in their lives.

The forms of social support available to the women vary greatly. Support comes from friends and family, bosses and teachers, social services counselors, and job training programs. Some women live in almost total isolation. Although they have their children and day-to-day activities, their lives are devoid of any other relationships, opportunities for positive feedback, or encouragement. Their options and opportunities are few. By contrast, other women are on forward paths thanks to steady and strong doses of positive and directed social support. Still others are able to keep going day-to-day because of support from friends or family.

Lives in Isolation

Some women live with almost no positive support, encouragement, or even words of praise. Not only are they cut off from knowledge of resources and opportunities, but even emotional support and friendships are minimal.

Leona, forty years old and the mother of five children, describes a life with almost no social support. She is the oldest of eight children. When she was young her father placed her with a foster family. She helped raise her brothers and sisters. She had her first child at sixteen.

"I just missed so much out of my life. There's never been someone there to talk to me if I have a problem. If something bothers me, I just kept it to myself. I just never had no one to actually talk to me. There's nothing like having a mother and a father. When they're not home, you just got to survive the best way you know how. So I survived the best way I knew how. At least a person can't say I didn't take care of my children, because I took care of them very well."

That Leona received little or no praise, encouragement, or support in her life is perhaps best shown by her response to the questions about people in her life who have helped and supported her.

"The only good person I remember was a woman named Sarah. I worked for her and her husband at PE fast-food place. They were so nice to me. I enjoyed what I was doing. And there was another lady. She was a business lady. I think she was working. She didn't have a business of her own, but she looked like a lady that was making good money. She said to me, 'If I had a business of my own, I would hire you right on the spot.' She was the only person I can remember that really had something to say to me that I would like to hear from other people. That was all a while ago."

The social isolation of many of the women can be illustrated by a brief description of the lives of Bobbie, Irene, and Sally.

Bobbie, thirty-two, lives alone in an apartment with her young son and baby. She works weekends as a barmaid/waitress and spends most of the rest of the time at home.

"I really don't have a lot of friends, just the associates I work with and the people that come in there. As far as people coming here or me doing things with friends, I don't. Any time I'm off work, I stay here with the kids."

Bobbie, like Leona, related only one incident of praise.

"My boss called me in the hospital. I was in the hospital for two weeks. I was in bad shape. She called to tell me she wished I would get back here. She said, 'No one's coming in because you aren't here. I need my number one barmaid back, then I can get my customers back.' That made me feel good."

Irene, thirty-three, has a son, nine. She is presently not working. *"I don't have no friends down here. I don't bother nobody. I pick my son up from school and go on in the house. That's about all we do. Then we do homework and watch TV."*

Sally, thirty-seven, lives with her two teenage children and a grandchild in a small trailer in a remote rural area. She has not worked for two years, partly because of poor health. She spends most of her daytime hours in the trailer, taking care of her grandchild. Her life has included two abusive marriages and difficulties with her children.

"I have some friends, but the one who was close to me moved away. No one really helps me, friends or family, but I usually talk to my mother when I know she is available. It's hard if something happens to you and you are by yourself. When I had this trouble with my legs, I got home and there was no one here and one vein busted. That was hard, not only scary, but hard. I try not to worry at all because it doesn't do a person any good to worry. Just take one day at a time. I'm not a worry person. I try not to worry about anything."

Bobbie, Irene, and Sally rarely interact with other people and are cut off from various forms of social support. They do not receive encouragement or understanding and have little knowledge of available opportunities and resources.

Vicki, Pat, and Emily engage somewhat more with friends or family. Although they are not as isolated as Bobbie, Irene, and Sally, they are alone often and find it difficult to seek or ask for help.

Vicki, thirty, lives with her two children in a semiconverted basement in her parents' home. She has lived there eight years, working full-time (until recently) during that period.

"I'm here all the time. I usually get out twice a week looking for jobs. I don't have a car. I can't afford to get mine fixed. My girlfriend picks me up. Sometimes we have lunch. Other than that, I'm just here raising my children. It makes like a dull life but I enjoy it.

"I just don't even think about getting out and socializing. I should though. I just don't have the time. It's in the evening and that's when I'm with my kids."

Pat, twenty-seven, is raising four children. *"Most friends don't stick around too long. My kids and my life are just too depressing or overwhelming for them. Maybe I'm doing more than they are but they are in a better situation than me so they don't like that, it is not comfortable. The money is tight, the children have come, and I just keep on going. In the midst of everything, I've gone back to school. The single parents that I have met, for one reason or another, are not like me. I would just as soon keep to myself."*

Emily, thirty-three, with four young children, is also without friends or supportive resources. She knows she needs job information and counseling help, but lack of child care impedes getting the former and lack of money prohibits the latter.

"I don't know. I really have no idea what I'm going to do. Actually, I really don't know what is out there to do, what kinds of jobs there are, what jobs entail. I feel very immature in that area.

"There is a program I can sign up for to help me get a career direction. I've talked with the girl quite a bit. I think in the spring I will be more comfortable leaving my youngest a little bit more. But I don't know who will take care of her. I don't have resources to call on and say 'help.' I don't even have a baby-sitter to go anywhere.

"I still feel stuck. The counseling I had was very helpful. It helped put it all together with all the why's and wherefore's. But I had to stop because I didn't have the money to continue paying, even though it was a sliding-scale fee. I could use it to help push me past where I am now to where I want to be, wherever that is.

"I'm not really the kind of person who gets together with friends a whole lot. I should do more of that. I think there is so much activity around here with the kids during the week that I just really like to be alone when I can."

Those who do not work are the most isolated. Their worlds are very narrow, focused on home life and the children. But even working does not guarantee a much broader range of support. The women go from home to work and then back home again. As marginalized workers, their employment does not draw them into a larger world or open doors of opportunity.

Isolation and the absence of encouragement and caring can exacerbate the difficult times. Its absence makes it much harder for the women to go forward. Without awareness of and access to opportunities, their options seem limited. Without some form of emotional support, praise, or caring, they can lose the strength necessary to fight, on a daily basis, the uphill battle.

Social Support: A Buffer and a Base

Social support comes in many forms. Bosses and teachers, job training programs, abuse shelter counselors, and friends, family, and church provide help, in small and large doses, to many of the women. Social support seems to serve as a buffer against fears, bolsters self-confidence and, for some, provides a base from which to pursue opportunities enabling them to leave poverty permanently.

Bosses and Teachers

A few women described a boss or teacher who had a positive influence on their efforts to maintain or develop in their role of provider.

Amelia, thirty-three, has two elementary-school-age children. *"I had a fantastic boss. Here's a good example. Both my children came down with chicken pox at the same time. It was like a nightmare. He said, 'Go ahead and use your annual leave.' I said, 'I can't leave the office that long.' So he said, 'Take a couple of days, and come back in, then if you need more time, take off again.'*

"So I stayed at home a few days, then came back in. The baby-sitter would call and say they are breaking out even more and I can't stop them from scratching, so I would need to go home again. He would tell me to go home, take care of the kids, and come back when they were not infected with chicken pox. So that was really good. He understood that I was by myself and there was nobody to help me. He was really great. There aren't a lot of bosses that are like that."

Marie, thirty-one, has three children in elementary school. *"I love my boss dearly. She is a wonderful lady. If I have sick children, she is very understanding. In any other job I probably would have gotten fired long ago because of sick kids. They have had tonsils out, tubes in the ears. But she is very understanding."*

Carol, the mother of three children, has just completed a two-year training program as a dental technician. *"I went to school every day, from 8:30 AM to 3:00 PM. My daughter was in kindergarten and day care, and then first grade. Most of the time she was in school, I was in school. It was hard, because when I first started she would hang on to me and cry and act like I was never coming back. What was really hard was my son. He was incarcerated at Sayles School and I was going back and forth to court for him. The school was a two-hour train ride each way and you could only go visit him during certain hours. The hours didn't coincide with my school hours. Because of him, I almost dropped out.*

"But my instructor encouraged me. She kept me at it, kept telling me everything was going to work out all right. Anytime that I missed or anything, I would bring her the court paper—she had a stack like this of court dates. When I graduated she said we should stick his picture on top. They are all my missed days, but I always managed to complete my projects.

"I always explained the whole situation to her and she understood. She said, 'Look, it's just a class. Everybody has their personal problems.' A lot of people got to the point where they dropped out, but she said to me, 'You've got to finish.' Miss Zinn made it real easy for me. She has kids of her own. I think that helped her to understand."

For some women, bosses and teachers helped provide career direction. Arlene has received her associate degree in business management. She went back to school to be a secretary, but a perceptive instructor changed her direction.

"I ran into some problems with my typing speed. One of the instructors, she encouraged me. She said I should go into business management. I looked at her and said, 'You don't know me. I am the most disorganized person there is.' She said, 'Well, that's just because you lack the skills. But you can learn.' That really stuck with me. I realized that you can do anything you want to, or be anything you want to be, if you are really determined enough. There is a whole library full of books. It's all just how serious you are about it. I changed my degree to business management."

Nancy, twenty-five, is working as an occupational therapist's aide. *"The therapist I work with kind of pushed me into going back to school and all. She said, 'Go for it.' The way she talked, once I graduate I will have a job with her. I'd like that. She is really nice."*

Several women described one teacher who helped build their confidence and self-esteem. These women had been or were enrolled in the same class and described the instructor as one providing very positive support.

Eva: *"Mr. Jerade makes you feel real good about yourself. He makes you feel comfortable. I'm going to take all his classes."*

Joy: *"Mr. Jerade is a great teacher. He cares about his students. He is just interested and listens to you. He makes me feel like I am doing something for myself. I'm definitely coming back for his math class."*

By providing an environment in which the women discovered they could learn, he inspired them to learn more. His expressions of concern and honest caring were what they needed to carry out their educational and work plans. These bosses and teachers provided social support at critical times in the lives of these women. Some provided support by minimizing the stress of the work and family balancing act. Others opened doors to new opportunities.

Job Training—With Some Extra Pluses

Another form of social support came through a federal- and state-funded job training program offered to impoverished single mothers. The program, called here the WT Program, is this state's version of the Job Opportunities and Basic Skills (JOBS) Training Program, created by the 1988 Family Support Act, which supports welfare-to-work programs. The state's WT Program provides training and educational assistance and help with transportation and child care while a woman pursues such training and education. Within sets of guidelines and monitored procedures, each service delivery provider, usually a county or merger of two or more counties, designs its own WT approach.

Seven of the women in the study had been enrolled in the WT Program in their area. With the help of the program, four of the women were able to return to school full-time and all four recently received associate degrees. Two women have completed their WT-sponsored educational and job training programs and are working part-time in their area of training. One woman is pursuing her associate degree and working part-time in her educational area.

All of the women benefited from the financial resources made available to them. They received tuition grants, monies toward car and child care expenses, along with the public assistance financial grants, food stamps, and medical coverage necessary for them to live on during their training years. Yet, as they told their stories, it was clear that it was the social support, within the WT Program or from particular case workers, that made the difference and facilitated their success. These forms of social support opened new windows of opportunity, enhanced their sense of self-esteem and self-worth, and were sources of emotional support and understanding.

Arlene, thirty-four, and the mother of three children, two in elementary school, recently completed two years of full-time schooling and received an associate degree in business management. *"I was on assistance for a little bit before the WT Program. Nobody ever told me about Pell grants or tried to give me information to better myself. I went into the system and, it's like, you can't get ahead. If you earn any money, they lower your benefits and you are just not getting anywhere.*

"But then they told me about the WT Program. I was really excited. It was a chance to get some kind of training. I went through the program. We were the first class. One of the speakers hired me as her receptionist. It was just part-time, but it gave me a chance to start overcoming some of my fears. I was so afraid of failure. I really kept myself down. It was a fear of failure, not having the confidence to think that I could do it.

"Before the program, I was down on myself really badly. I didn't know the first step to take. I didn't know where to go, who to contact, what I was doing, or anything. The WT Program showed me a lot. In fact, in our class, a representative came from the business college and spoke to our class. I think that was what put the bug in my head about the business college."

Susan, in her early twenties, is raising a young son and is now a certified nurse's aide. *"I was trying to get off welfare, get help with my GED, and the job training and the whole bit. I called but was told there was a waiting list because the class was already filled for the year. So a year later I got a call and they asked me if I was still interested in WT. I went and had an interview, told them I was interested, and it just got started from there. The next week I was working on my GED and my basic skills.*

"WT has been just great. They have really been there to help me through anything. They help you get a car, they help you with day care. If you don't have transportation, they even helped me with a taxi for a while. It's as if you go in with a problem, they are always understanding. They have been really great.

"I wanted to be more than who I was. I didn't want to be the shy, timid little girl who sat around and waited for the welfare check. Mostly what got me started was my ambition. I wanted to be more. I just knew I needed the right support system behind me to get me off my rear and get out there and get it done.

"And that was WT. We had a six-week workshop on esteem. A couple of the girls in the class were battered as wives. We had a workshop on all of that and it helped to really build up to who I am now. Back then, if you would be here right now, I wouldn't have said two words. When I was growing up, my mother always told me, 'You will never be nothing.' Well, that's just not true."

Julie, in her thirties and the mother of two elementary school children, just completed two years of full-time college-level education. She lost her job shortly after leaving her husband and had to go on public assistance.

"When I went in I told them, 'I don't want to be on welfare, but this is the only option I have. Are there any training programs, educational programs, to get me out of welfare?' The intake worker said, 'Don't worry about it. There is nothing. Stay on welfare until your youngest is six.' It wasn't true. The only reason I found out about the WT Program was that I was going through the blue pages trying to get heat assistance. I found the number for the JTPA (Job Training and Partnership Act) Job Training office and got in the WT Program through the back door.

"When I first entered the program, I was really afraid I would fail. I had failed at my marriage. I had failed at being a daughter, thought I was failing as a mother. So I thought, 'They are giving me this opportunity. What happens if I fail?'

"Starting the program, that was really hard for me. I'm not one to speak about my problems. I was raised where you keep everything inside. All the skills they taught me were very helpful. How to dress, all about nutrition. I didn't know anything about nutrition. It was extremely helpful to learn about things other people take for granted.

"Before the WT Program I thought that minimum-wage jobs were all that I could ever get or do. But then I found out how intelligent I was. Through JTPA I took some intelligence tests and had one of the highest scores. It seemed like, 'Okay, I can do this.' I've always wanted to go to college but I always felt I couldn't do it. So then I started doing brushup. I was willing to try. That willingness I think is what got me started. I had an inner drive that I didn't know I had until all this with WT and everything came about. I'm going from a person that has been browbeaten all of her life to somebody that is emerging out of her shell.

"The other turning point came for me after I was in school. It was like a three-ring circus. I have the children, five classes, driving back and forth. It was quite a struggle to juggle all of that. I realized that I couldn't do this on my own. I could ask for help and not feel disgraced. The case worker was able to do things that I couldn't do, like straighten out my schedule. I didn't feel disgraced after the help came. I didn't feel like I was a failure.

"I realized that there are people out there that care. They helped me. Then it got better. I knew there were people that I could call, that I had the support that I needed, that these people understood what I was going through."

The WT Program did more for these women than provide basic resources. They entered with limited knowledge and left aware of a much wider range of possibilities for their lives. They came into the program with fear and a low sense of self-worth. They are all now on a journey of self-discovery and self-development. They felt alone. They found help, understanding, and the support they needed to begin moving themselves and their children out of poverty.

Of the seven women in the WT Program, three recounted how they had to seek it out. Arlene was in the system for a while before she was told about it. Susan called and then was put on a one-year waiting list. And Julie was discouraged from applying until her children were older. Yet each woman persisted and now all three are in or are on their way to employment opportunities that can lead them out of poverty permanently. The stereotypical view of women on public assistance is that they are lazy and unmotivated. Another commonly held view is that the welfare system has to "push" women off of it. These stories suggest otherwise. It was the women who took the initiative. And when they did, it was not necessarily encouraged, and, in one case, was discouraged. While the program was a door to opportunities, the door was sometimes locked or hidden from view.

Abuse Shelters

Not all of the women who experienced abusive relationships went to shelters for battered women. Some just left the relationship and continued with their lives. Those who used the services of a shelter did, for the most part, find the shelter services helpful.

The women who went to the shelters needed the safety and protection from the abuser that the shelter offered. Amelia, Emily, and Gloria experienced severe physical abuse and the shelter was a necessary haven.

Amelia was severely beaten by her husband. *"I went to the hospital and the police took my children to a shelter for abused women and children. We had to stay six weeks until they knew that he couldn't find us because they knew he wasn't going to get any more jail sentence. We stayed there for six weeks and that was really nice, except that I had two black eyes, a busted nose, and a swollen up face."*

In addition to safety, some shelters offer counseling services. Gloria's husband physically abused her and sexually abused their four daughters. *"The counseling was very helpful, because I had a lot of guilt. How could I let this happen to my children? I'm the mother. They helped me to understand that I didn't see it. I can see it now, but I couldn't then.*

"I was really surprised to see how many women had gone through a lot of the same experiences I had. It helped to talk about it. I thought of starting a

support group, but nobody had the extra time. Everyone had families and home and school. A lot of them had had counseling or were in counseling. It did help us to talk about it."

The shelter was the only place Emily, who then had three young children, could go to escape from her abusive husband. But she had needs that she wished had been met by the shelter. *"It's short term. While you are there you have to go looking for apartments and go to the agencies to see what you can get. Most of the time you don't get all that you need. That's why so many of us end up back in the abusive relationship.*

"There is a real need for the women to be nurtured and told the truth constantly about themselves. What would be really good is to have long-term shelters for women where you can just stay and stay and get job help."

Jean experienced mental abuse and potential physical abuse. The shelter made it possible for her, with five children to take care of, to leave her marriage. She was fortunate that her shelter also offered a one-year housing opportunity, not unlike what Emily was looking for. *"While I was at the shelter they don't let you sit around, they get you moving. I started my classes for my GED. Then I went through a job search. When I finished my GED classes I took a computer course. Then I was placed in a temporary clerical job for six months.*

"I have to give the shelter credit for getting me back on my feet. They gave me the self-confidence and motivation I needed to get out there and get on my own. I have to give them credit for that. Nancy was my counselor when I started there and she was the best. Any little thing you did, like registering your child at day care, and you got a pat and a hug came from her. She was great. She made you feel good."

Family, Friends, and Her Church

Some of the women received support from more traditional sources: family, friends, and church. For the most part, this support was less directed than job training or help with abuse. Most families and friends were not able to provide financial support. Rather, traditional sources usually could simply be counted on to "be there" for the women.

Several women spoke in warm, positive tones about the importance of their mother or grandmother in their lives.

Jessie: *"My mom helps me out a lot. I don't know what I would do without her. She lives on social security and doesn't have much money. She's pretty much homebound and doesn't go anywhere. But I'll call her and tell her what's happening. If I need cigarettes or something minor, she helps me out with that. Emotional support—she is there. She is a great help. I wouldn't be able to make it without her."*

Sheila: *"My mother was very supportive towards me. She still is supportive. She stuck by me. She tells me, 'Don't worry, things will work out.' If I don't talk to her everyday, it's like I lose something. She always asks, 'How did your day go? Did you find a job?' Or she has an idea for a job. I try to get to see her at least twice a week."*

Joy: *"After my mom died it was kind of hard, but my grandmother was always there for me. She helped me. She basically has been there all my life. She just guided me through, and my grandfather."*

Some women had very supportive families—parents or siblings or both.

Arlene: *"My family is a very, very big part of my life. When we do get together, when any of us sisters get together, or if I take the kids and spend the night with my mom, when we get together I can't even describe the feeling. It's such a wonderful feeling to spend time with my sisters because we don't get to do it that often.*

"I told my sister when I graduated that I owed much of it to her. My sister helped me out with the baby-sitting. She would pick them up [my kids] from day care, feed them supper, and give them baths. Then she would bring them to my house, put them to bed, and wait for me to get home, usually around 9:30."

A few women described friends who were supportive and encouraging.

Susan: *"My big supporters are my best friend and my fiancé. They are really big supporters of me. My best friend, she was in college. She wanted to be a lab technician, but she quit and works at Smith Company. She is always telling me, 'Don't give up, don't give up, don't quit.' "*

Arlene: *"I have a good friend in Florida. She had more faith in me than I had in myself. She used to tell me how strong she thought I was. She doesn't even know I have this job because I can't afford to call long distance. When I write her, she is going to be very proud of me. She encouraged me to go to school, she always encouraged me to go to school."*

Renata, thirty-seven, with two teenage children, spoke of the positive support she has received from her church.

Renata: *"I just got tired of trying to fix things and nothing would get fixed. Things would change and I couldn't change them back. I started going to church and I ended up going and going. I started going a year ago and am getting to know a lot of people. I was the type that stayed home all the time. I went to work, came home, went to work, came home. I didn't associate with many people on the block. I had one neighbor on one side and a girlfriend on the other, and that was it. Now I go to church every Sunday, I sing in the choir, and I talk to people all day long.*

"One women said, 'You look so good, you have a glow, it's your aura. I don't know what it is but you look so different.' A little old lady that lives up the street also said, 'You should have started going to church a long time ago—you look good.' It all gives me a little bit more confidence each day. If I can make it this day, then I can make it the next day and the next one and the next one."

The Role of Social Support

Sources and forms of social support the women described include: 1) encouragement, praise for doing well, and caring people; 2) teachers, and bosses who understand their lives and are willing to be flexible; and 3) social systems that demonstrate an understanding of their needs by providing relevant support, such as transportation and child care. Also important are opportunities to learn about and gain access to job-related resources. For many, discovering they have talents, that there are jobs and educational opportunities open to them, and finding out how to tap into these opportunities are as important as emotional support. Both encouragement and awareness of opportunities are important types of social support. Finally, counseling, such as in the shelters, also helps to put their experiences in perspective.

The most fortunate women in the study seemed to be those in the WT Program. The program, especially when it was combined with group work or classes with other WT women, clearly provided a social support group, as well as job-related resources. One WT participant referred frequently to "we WT girls." WT's combination of emotional and resource support enabled the women to overcome fears, struggle onward despite many hurdles—car breakdowns, sick children, and intensive schoolwork—and complete their programs of study.

Social support is not the answer to all their problems and difficult circumstances. It doesn't pay the rent or provide food. Nor can one form of support necessarily compensate for another. Yet each form of support provides some bolstering. Family support, for example, may not provide financial or job help, but it can keep a woman going. Anita, with a strong family support system, has a very upbeat attitude toward life. *"My motto is, If there's a will, there's a way."* Although she has not pinpointed a long-term career, this support can fuel her emotionally until she can find the job resources. Renata found support in church and that keeps her in school while she works for her GED. The common denominator of all forms of social support is that it provides hope. In one way or another, it keeps the women's vision of a better future for themselves and their children in the forefront and encourages them to keep moving forward.

EIGHT. I Used to Have Dreams

During the interviews, the women expressed their views on several specific topics. Some women spoke directly about the positive and negative aspects of the welfare system. Others expressed strong opinions about the courts and the child-support payment system. Many voiced frustrations with obtaining adequate housing and reliable transportation. Finally, all of the women were asked about their dreams for the future.

The Welfare System: Option of Necessity, Not Choice

As the women's stories indicate, they applied for public assistance out of necessity, not out of choice. These women are in precarious positions because of their lack of education and job skills and the betrayal by the mate. Any negative event, such as being fired from a job, a sick child needing attention, or health problems, can push them over the edge into poverty. Welfare becomes their only survival option.

Survival, Not Living

None of the women described being on welfare as a satisfactory way to live and raise a family. Indeed, the cash grant, and even the grant and the food stamps, cannot bring a woman and her family up to the poverty level. The cash and food stamp allowances are about 70 percent of the poverty level, providing just bare subsistence for the families.

Renata: *"The hardest part about living on welfare and juggling money is paying the bills. They give you enough to survive on but they don't give you enough to live on. There is a difference. They don't think so, but there is."*

Susan: *"Welfare is designed to keep you where you were ten years earlier."*

Marilyn: *"My main thing with welfare is, it's not hard to get on it and it's not hard to go off it, but it's hard to get something out of it while you are on it."*

Carol: *"Between the food stamps and the cash grant, I just about make it. If you make partial payments on your bills, you can manage. Other than that, there is no way it covers other things you need, especially when the kids need clothes for school."*

Some, like Arlene and Amelia, see welfare as a dead-end system.

Arlene: *"I went into the system and it's like, you can't get ahead. If you earn money, they lower your benefits, and you are just not getting anywhere."*

Amelia: *"When I was working, at five dollars an hour, they prorated my AFDC checks down to seventy-nine dollars a month. But this is what I don't understand. When they prorate your check down, your food stamps go way up. I don't understand. I can't pay my bills, but my food is there."*

But there are no other options for the women.

Connie: *"If it hadn't been there, I would have been in a very desperate situation. I don't know what I would have done. You need the assistance."*

Anita: *"I get a medical card for her and I get food stamps. If it wasn't for them, I wouldn't be able to do it, to tell you the truth."*

Vicki: *"I had to leave my job because of medical problems. I tried to get on unemployment, but I couldn't. So I've been looking for work. I had no choice but to go on assistance."*

Feelings of Shame and Degradation

Many of the women talked about how badly they feel about themselves for being on welfare.

Ursula: *"I used to feel downcast for being on welfare. It was something I felt low-rated about. It felt degrading. They want to know who is giving you this or who is helping to send your child to school. If I had to stop paying the water bill this month to keep them in school for the next month, I would do that. But that's my business. I don't like them prying into what somebody may give me or who is paying something for me."*

Joy: *"When you are on public assistance, it's like you're going to pick up someone else's money that you didn't work for. You didn't make it yourself. When I got my first welfare check it felt odd, because I could compare it to receiving my work check. I knew what it was like to have both. I used to hear people say, 'Well, you are taking money from people that work and you are not working.' It felt kind of funny to be a person on the other side this time. This is my first experience with welfare. Nobody in my household had ever been on public assistance but me. My mother worked for the government and so did my grandmother. I was the first person that ever needed welfare.*

"I don't like the people who work in the welfare offices. They are nasty to me. They have a bad attitude. They act real snooty and they really don't want to do the work. They act like the money is coming right out of their pockets. I figure, if I go in there with a nice attitude, because I know some people are nasty with them, too, then they will be different. But it doesn't help. They still are nasty."

Susan: *"I used to feel like I was just this tall. I just felt like I just was wee little. It was being on welfare plus everything that I've been through. Like the welfare image. If you take food stamps to the store, you get looks like, 'Oh my God.' I'm glad that I'm done with all of that."*

Marie: *"You get this little card and then you show it and you get your food stamps. It's kind of degrading. When you go into the grocery store you hope nobody from work sees you standing in the line with food stamps. But then, on the other hand, I do work. It's not like I'm sitting at home and taking handouts. I do work. If I didn't work, I would feel like it's a handout. But I do work and I can't make it, so I deserve to have that help. That's the way I feel. And my kids deserve that."*

LaVerne: *"I really don't care anymore about being on welfare. You gotta do what you gotta do. I have a child to take care of and if I have to do that to take care of her, then I'm going to do it.*

"It doesn't make me feel bad anymore, like it used to. I used to hate to go to the grocery store and give out my food stamps. But now it just doesn't bother me."

Welfare as a Safety Net

Those women for whom doors of opportunity are beginning to open are looking forward to the day when they will no longer be on welfare.

Carol, on full benefits, recently completed a two-year dental technician program. She has three children. *"Soon I hope to be working in the field I'm trained and saying bye-bye to welfare. And it will be never too soon, believe me."*

But some of the women voiced concerns about losing the safety net that welfare provides.

Carol: *"Right now I'm looking for a job, but if I get any kind of job you got to think about health benefits because it's not going to cover what a medical card covers. When you get a job you say bye-bye to food stamps, which is then money coming out of your pay. It seems like when you start with the work world it seems like you give up a lot more than you get. When you turn around, you got to pay day care and transportation, which right now they are giving me. You got to pay for food. God forbid one of your kids gets sick and you don't have coverage. What do you do then? Right now you got a medical card."*

Marie, with three children, works thirty hours a week and receives food stamps and a temporary medical card from public assistance. She is planning to go to work full-time, but, like Carol, is anxious about the trade-offs and fears losing the safety net.

Marie: *"I just put in for full time. Now I'm a little scared. I don't want to go in the hole. I don't. But I decided I've really got to try on my own, so I put in for full time. Which will mean, I don't know. I don't know if I will be eligible for food stamps, then that will have to come out of my pocket. You see, then my rent will go up and then my child care will go up. So am I going to make it?*

"I'm not sure how it will affect everything. If I could see into the future and see that, hey, it's going to be okay. But you don't know until you try it. I don't know if I can afford three kids and all those bills. I'm afraid of change, I guess. One thing with welfare, you can count on it. You get familiar with the kind of income you are going to have. Although they never give you enough food stamps, it's a sure steady thing."

Julie, with two children and full benefits, has finished her associate degree and is looking for a job. She welcomes a gradual, rather than a rapid termination of welfare benefits.

"If I get the job I interviewed for this morning, I won't be completely off the system immediately. I will be on cash assistance for three months, they will adjust it, unless it pays something like twelve dollars an hour. During the three-month period I will pay day care myself. Then once cash assistance is closed, they will pick up a part of my baby-sitting fees for up to a year. I'll probably be on food stamps for at least another year, depending on the wages. There will be a blue medical card for myself and my children, if I have to pay the medical.

"The support is there, no matter where I'm at. They said I will probably be in the system in one form or another for the next three years. They don't expect you to get a twelve-dollar-an-hour job. Most of us will be making six or seven dollars an hour.

"So it's gradual. People aren't going to just drop you. That's one thing that people don't understand. You are used to getting this paycheck every two weeks, getting your food stamps once a month, and your medical bills are paid. Then you are asking us to drop all of this within a couple of weeks. We can't do it. It's just not psychologically right. We need to know that there is somebody back there because of the fear that haunts most of us. Now most of the girls on public assistance, I don't know any of them that don't have some kind of dysfunction in their past, so they need that extra support."

One interpretation of Carol, Marie, and Julie's concerns might be that of "welfare dependence." But another look at their concerns within the context of their lives suggests that their fears and anxieties are quite legitimate. Marie's pay will increase to about $18,000 per year. She has three young children and is still paying off her husband's debts. Julie, with two young children, will start at around $14,000 per year. These incomes bring them only slightly above the poverty level. None of these women have families who can provide any financial support, should they need it, nor do they now have any savings to speak of or other significant assets. They are the sole providers for their families and look ahead to salaries that may rise somewhat, but so will the expenses of their children and living costs. It would seem that most anyone with the sole financial and parenting responsibility would be anxious about taking away a safety net too rapidly, going in the financial hole, having no money for emergency situations, or ending up even worse off than before. For women starting out at low salary levels, with no assets or financial backup, fear and concern are very appropriate responses. While welfare provides very little, as Marie said, "you could count on it." For most women in the study, there was very little else they could count on. Most decidedly, it was not the father of their children.

None of the women on public assistance sounds like a welfare queen. The women need welfare, are forced by circumstances to accept it, see no way off of it, or hope to get off as soon as possible. But no one likes it or appears to gain from it, other than those who are enrolled in educational and work training programs. Many feel degraded and "low rated" for being on welfare. Few recognize and value their survival skills. They carry on their shoulders the weight of society's negative stereotype of welfare women.

Child-Support Payments

Only thirteen of the thirty women receive child support on a regular basis. Of these thirteen women, eight are on full assistance (cash grant, food stamps, and medical). These eight women are entitled to receive only fifty dollars per month in child support over the public assistance amount, regardless of the amount paid to the state by the father. The remainder goes to the state to offset the cash-grant AFDC payments.

Some were confused about the fifty dollar payment.

Vicki: *"I just started getting child support. My husband never paid support all these years. I found out that he was working. I am supposed to get twenty-two dollars a week, eleven dollars for each child, but I don't get it. So far, I haven't gotten nothing. I figure welfare is taking it because I am getting assistance from them. But I have only been on welfare now for three months."*

Others disagreed with the welfare system's approach to child-support payments.

Amelia: *"My husband was court-ordered to pay child support every week. He makes good money. It took fourteen months to find him. But I can't get the child support. Sometimes I get a fifty dollar passthrough check a month.*

"They did say I was due some refunds because I had been skipped over so much. I said, 'I don't understand why are you people keep picking on me? I'm out of work. I have been out of work for three months.' They explained that I was only getting fifty dollars because I was getting a full cash grant, the max. I told them, 'If you want to send me my child support, you can keep your food stamps. Or you can keep me on food stamps and I'll take my child support every week and you can have your AFDC back and give it to another needy family.' They won't do that. You can't fight the system."

The welfare system of child-support payments to the women produced confused reactions or disagreements about the approach. But it was the court system and the enforcement system that elicited the strongest negative reactions.

Susan: *"I didn't get child support for a long time. I think enforcement services doesn't do what they are supposed to do. I don't believe they do. When he wasn't paying they kept sending me letters saying, 'We are going to have a bench warrant for his arrest.' He never even showed for those hearings. He was supposed to and he isn't in jail. They don't get tough. I'd like to go in there some time when they say that and just laugh at them and say 'Where is my son's money?' "*

Carol: *"I don't get child support. You can't find these wayward men. One time I actually gave them his address and everything and they never followed through. You've got to keep going to court and more or less keep pressing charges for it. But it all takes time out of your time and it seems like they don't follow up with it anyway."*

Jessie: *"I don't get child support. It is court-ordered, but they don't know where he is. I know where he is. He is in a VA hospital. The courts know where he is, but they choose not to go after him. He owes me over five thousand dollars. He doesn't have any money. What's the point, I guess, is how they look at it. They could throw him in jail, but that ain't going to get me any money either. I don't know what he is doing. He ain't helping me, I know that."*

Sally: *"I get a fifty-dollar support payment from assistance if my husband pays child support. I had to fight for it though. I had to take him to court several times to get it. I had a hard time getting it. I had to get a lawyer and all. If you leave it to the state, it will take forever."*

Julie: *"Child support, that's the one complaint I have with the system. I was in enforcement services less than six weeks after leaving a marriage that was potentially explosive. I am still very frightened of this man. I didn't know which end is up. I'm going against all that I believe in. You know, that you don't leave a marriage, that type of situation. And I'm facing this woman who wants to sock him for every penny. I'm sitting there frightened to death with no counsel, no legal counsel whatsoever. And he's sitting there with me. All he had to do was look at me and I'm afraid. So he was able, in that sense, to talk the child support down to one hundred sixty dollars a month for the two children and it is still at that. The state gets the one hundred sixty dollars and I get fifty of that.*

"Now maybe not all women who are leaving their husbands or boyfriends are as frightened as I am. But I feel there should be some legal counsel or protection when you go into enforcement services. That's my biggest complaint."

When the ex-mate had disappeared and couldn't be found, or was not working, because of alcohol or drug addiction or, in the case of Gloria's husband, because he was in jail, child support was not an issue. But the main complaint of women with former mates who were working or could be working, was with the system for not helping them obtain the support due to their children. There was a general feeling that the enforcement system was lax, did not always operate in their best interests, and rarely imposed sanctions on these men who failed to pay or appear in court.

Lacking the Basics: Housing and Transportation

Some women were frustrated with their attempts to find adequate housing. For others, a major hardship was the lack of money for a car or car maintenance. These concerns were, unlike other concerns, related to living in a city versus living in a small town or rural location. While all of the women were concerned with housing, the city women were far more dissatisfied and frustrated with their efforts to find adequate housing than those in towns and rural areas. Transportation, however, was less an issue for the city women than it was for many of the women living in small towns and rural areas.

Housing Neighborhoods

Unlike the small-town and rural women, many city women spoke about safety and crime in their neighborhoods, suggesting that the city setting exacerbates the harshness of their lives.

Leona: *"Where I live there's lots of guns, shooting, and stuff like that, lots of drugs and stuff. It's scary."*

Sheila: *"Where I live now is fairly safe, but you still have a little drugs. We just don't go outside. I'm in the house by nine, my doors shut. Nobody can come to the house after nine o'clock. That's a rule with me and it's a rule with the people I know. They're scared.*

"My street is nice, but two blocks away, that's where you have all your happenings. You never know who is going to come up on your back. You can't trust people. You don't want to walk your children through that neighborhood, though that's where you have to catch a bus. During the daytime it's okay, but after five o'clock—no, no."

Renata: *"If it's nice outside, we would go outside on the step. I like to do that, but our neighborhood is really not that good. A while ago, there were some boys that used to live up the street. They were like into drugs and stealing cars. They were always coming through the streets shooting stuff."*

Housing Assistance and Waiting Lists

Through the Department of Housing and Urban Development (HUD), low-income people are able to get into housing, termed Section 8 housing, for which part of their rent is subsidized. Small-town, rural, and urban women all expressed frustrations with being on the subsidized housing waiting list for years. More small-town and rural than urban women, however, had received help from the HUD program.

Jean, in a small town, was able to obtain adequate housing for herself and her five children with the help of rental assistance. *"The rent is supposed to be $540 a month, but I'm paying $169 a month because housing kicks in the rest. I moved in here a month before my voucher came through because I knew I was on the top of the list and it was only a matter of time. CAP paid half of the first month's rent and I had to come up with the other half. The finances are out there if you know where to look for them. The women's shelter was pretty good about giving you the information."*

For Arlene, also living in a town, help with housing facilitated her moving out of poverty. *"With three kids and nowhere to turn, for a little while I lived with my sister. Then I got into the housing project and that's the only thing that saved me as far as housing. I did not have the money to rent a house or pay for a security deposit and all that stuff. But the housing helped me a lot. I will probably be on my way out of here soon so someone else can come in, now that I got my new job and I'm very happy now."*

Emily lives with her four young children in a town. She is hoping her housing situation will improve shortly. *"This apartment is partially subsidized. The rent is $325 a month, which is not what I think of as subsidized. I lived in another town on subsidized housing where my rent was $82 a month. I have been on a Section 8 waiting list now for four years. I'm number ten now. Maybe in another six months to a year it will be my turn. Then my rent will be 30 percent of my income. That will really ease things. I'll be able to buy my children shoes or I can get myself a pair of shoes. All the normal things are luxuries now."*

But Eva and Sheila, both living in a city, have never received any housing assistance and do not foresee any subsidized housing becoming available in the near future.

Eva: *"I live with my grandmother. I would really like to be on my own with my two children. I have been on the Section 8 waiting list for six years. They said it might be another year or two. Every time you call them, they tell you to just wait until you get something in the mail. They won't talk to you or anything."*

Sheila: *"The hardest part was when I left my husband and couldn't find a place to live. I went to get an apartment. I couldn't get an apartment. I went to housing. I couldn't get housing. It was the line, the list was long. They wanted to put you in the projects, and I was never raised up in the projects and I was very scared. That was the hardest time. Still today I can't get a HUD house because they are overextended or overcrowded. The list is long."*

Housing Bureaucracies

City women also expressed frustration with housing agency bureaucracies, and two of the ten city women had at one time lived in homeless shelters with their children. City women clearly had more bureaucracies to deal with and even shelter life had bureaucratic complications.

Carol describes her efforts to keep and fix up her house. *"Right now I'm fighting the city for three years for my house. I was renting it originally, then the owner gave it to me. They give it away because they can't keep up with the taxes and the water bills and so on. But that was like four years ago and I'm still waiting for the deed. Now these people, you got to stay on them constantly, and when you are busy going to school and doing everything else, by the time you get there, they are gone from their offices.*

"Meanwhile the house is a mess. It rained through my entire house for a good six months. It started in the bathroom, moved to the hallway, the bedrooms. I mean it completely and utterly rained through my house.

"Now I'm not responsible for anything until I get the papers. But the landlord is no longer responsible, nobody is. They got grants all over the city that can help you fix this and help you fix that, but you need the deed. I'm a homeowner, but I'm not. I go to the fourth floor for one thing and the tenth for another and then the tenth floor sends you back to the fourth floor to get a paper, so you come back down. This city is really weird when it comes to these things.

"Half of my ceilings are down. I've got plumbing that leaks and lead pipes. Believe me, I've become a plumber and an electrician. I want a heater because I have been using kerosene heat for the last three years. But to me, we've lived in that house since my oldest son was two years old. To me that is what you call home. That's why I'm fighting so hard to keep it. Then it will be mine and then it will be my children's."

Eva, twenty-two, with two young children, describes her experiences with shelters for the homeless. *"This year I went in a shelter. I got tired of arguing with my grandmother. So we went to a shelter for a month, and I left because it was so dirty. If you are in a shelter, they place you like day-to-day, in different places, every day. Sometimes you are sleeping in the basement of a church.*

"By going to shelter to shelter each day, you have to be in their office every day, so you can't go look for a job or do what you need to do to help yourself more. You have to be there to talk to a counselor every day. I could take my son to school but I had to get someone to pick him up because most of the time I wouldn't be out of there until like five or six at night. The majority of the time if you don't have all your kids with you at the time, they only place you and the kid that's with you. It was wild.

"I can't live like that, so I went back with my grandmother. In most of the good shelters you have your own room, you have a basin in the room. But it's a long waiting list."

Adequate housing is a basic necessity. For poor women raising children alone, substandard housing, constant rent money worries, or frequent moves drain energies and make it even harder to deal with all the other difficulties in their lives.

Transportation

If women in the city are worn down by housing issues, the lives of women in small towns and rural areas are often circumscribed by the lack of adequate transportation. Most directly affected are their employment situations.

Jessie: *"I don't have transportation now. That's my main problem. If I had a car, I know I could get a job in the next town because opportunities are there. Also, I've been to the job training office. She believes there is some help available. If I get a job first, she thinks there is some kind of assistance towards a car. So the only problem is, how do you get out there and look without transportation to go look? It is kind of a catch-22. My daughter and I were going job hunting together, but now she doesn't have a car anymore either. Then my brother was letting me use his, but then he sold it. So I've been kind of stuck. Right now, all I have to ride is my bike or my horse. If they just had hitching posts like they used to, I'd ride my horse everywhere."*

Vicki: *"I have a car but it is not working. It takes money to get that fixed. I have a girlfriend that comes up twice a week and we go job hunting. If I need to be somewhere, she will come and get me."*

Amelia: *"One of the biggest barriers getting work is the distance with this car. It is thirteen years old. I do the tires. I do the oil. As long as you keep all that going, she runs. I'm afraid if I work any further away with the car being so old, I'm going to get stuck."*

Arlene was in the WT Program and drove back and forth to school for over two years.

Arlene: *"I had some help from WT with car costs and that was another roadblock that was knocked down for me. I wouldn't say totally because they helped some, but it was limited help. But I've always had junk cars. You know how it is with junk cars, you experience all that stuff. All of the little emergencies, unexpected fix ups that you don't have the money for. I was set back so many times, sometimes I just sit back and I am amazed that I made it through. One automobile problem could set me back for a couple of months. It would take me that long to get back on track financially.*

"I would like to get a loan someday to get me a decent, a reliable car. I have always just had junk cars, problem-pain-in-the-butt cars, and I've always wanted to feel what it was like to have a nice car."

Other aspects of their lives, in particular parenting responsibilities, are also affected by a lack of a car.

Jessie: *"My daughter ran her hand through the wringer of the washer last week and I needed to take her to the hospital. I called everybody and finally got in touch with my daughter and she came over and took us. She was okay, nothing was broken, but it is a scary feeling when you have children and they get hurt and you don't have any transportation."*

Cars are considered basic necessities for life outside of the city. But for poor women in small towns and rural areas, it is one more necessity that they have to worry about. They can only afford old cars in need of repairs, which often overstretch the budget, and the car may not be usable for periods of time. They need a car to look for a job, and a job to pay for the car and its maintenance. Simple chores, like shopping, become major events, and minor emergencies become times of worry and anguish. The number of "what if" accidents or places to be that you can't be without a car add to their already long list of difficulties and concerns.

Dreams for the Future

The women were asked about their dreams for themselves. What were *their* dreams, as opposed to dreams for their children? Where did they see their lives going in the next several years? For some, the question came as a surprise, as if no one had asked them that question in a very long time. For others, it was a struggle to answer. They had not allowed themselves the luxury of having dreams of their own. Their focus was on their children and on just making it from day to day. For some, there was pain in remembering lost dreams. But most women still had dreams, and their eyes were on the future as they described these hopes for themselves and their children.

Dreams for Myself?

Some women appeared not to have dreams for the future. One expressed her dream, but then described it as an impossible one. Others were hesitant or surprised at the question, but eventually chose to reveal some of their dreams.

Judy: *"What do I think about for the future? What do I dream about? Nothing, nothing. I like waitress work. I do. I was good in art in school. I used to get those magazines where you draw pictures for scholarships. I used to do them all the time when I was young. But I never sent them in."*

Sally: *"I'd like to find Mr. Right. Which seems like it ain't going to happen because everybody is about the same. I mean every guy I met always had some faults. I have my faults, too. But it seems like all the ones I meet end up abusive."*

Leona: *"My dream? I don't think my mind can go that far. I'm still trying to work on right now. I'd like to see a plaque sitting on my wall saying, 'Leona W———, college graduate, student."*

Emily: *"What do I want to be? Gosh, I don't allow myself the luxury to think of these things. It's a luxury to think of things about myself in any other way than I am now. What I have to do is survive. I can't think about what I want to be.*

"I'm just trying to survive. I've been trying to emotionally survive and physically survive. We aren't as bad off as many. We have our basic needs met. But to have all your dreams crumble around you in the last decade. I can't allow myself—I don't know if that's right or not—I can't allow myself to dream, not allow myself to think about what it could be like, what it might be like."

Vicki: *"My dreams? I used to have dreams. I used to have dreams but . . . I'd like to find somebody that I could love again and who could love me. That I more or less do want to be a family, like husband and wife. That gets to me at times. I try not to let it bother me, but it does get to me at times. And I'd like to hold down a good job. I'd really like to have my own nursing home and have my children there to help me."*

The voices of all these women are sad. They see their lives as staying the same. They don't believe they can get and hold on to what they want—like love and a family. To dream is to risk wanting and not getting. Women like Sally, Emily, and Vicki have already experienced many broken dreams. It may be too painful for them to dream anymore.

Dreaming Out of Poverty

The majority of the women were able to envision a better future for themselves and their children.

Susan: *"In seven or eight years I will probably be a licensed practical nurse. I'll be driving my new Camaro. I'll have land and a house. I'm only twenty-two. I just want to be a real nurse and have things I've always wanted and my kids to have things that they've always wanted. I can remember when I was growing up, all I heard was 'we really can't afford it.' I had to hear that all my life and I don't want it to happen to my kids."*

Nancy: *"In seven years I hope I will be living in my log cabin house. Not the wooden ones, but the newer ones. I'd like a new car and everything in the house to be new. The way my boss talks about my work as an occupational therapist, I'll be able to afford all of this stuff. That's what I want, everything."*

Eva: *"I just want to be living comfortably and have money in my pockets every day or in the bank, just to feel comfortable. The main thing is money. I really need a job."*

Carla: *"I'd like to have my own house. Not just for myself but for the kids, so when I'm gone, at least I know I left them a house. I'd like to be comfortable. I never really wanted to be rich or powerful or anything like that. I just want to be comfortable. I want my kids to have what they want and need and for me to have a nice home, a nice car, some money in the bank. I don't want fancy cars, or a mansion or to be famous or anything like that. Just to be comfortable."*

Dreaming the American Dream

The dreams of most of the women are basic—a home, a job, a car, some financial security, perhaps a mate, family happiness, and some simple pleasures.

A Home of Her Own

Jean: *"I'd like to have my own home sometime, really. I'd like to move out of town. I want a yard. I want country."*

Meg: *"I would like to have my own house."*

Anita: *"I think my biggest wish is to own my own home. I would like a farmhouse. I'd rather live in the country. I know it will take me a while and it will take a lot of work to get there. I want a nice home, even if it is a fixer-upper. I don't care about that. I like getting my hands dirty. I like to paint. I painted this whole apartment. I really enjoy working in my yard. I would really like to live on a farm. I love animals. That would make me content."*

Vocational Dreams

Others dreamed of better jobs, careers, or opportunities for further schooling.

Connie: *"I'm going for my associate's degree. But I would like to get my bachelor's in nursing. I want to be an OR nurse. I want to work in surgery. I find it fascinating."*

Marie: *"What I would really like to do is go to school and become a nurse."*

Renata: *"In seven years I'm going to have my own restaurant. I'm going to own it. My daughter, she is going to be established and my son will be finished with school and will own his own construction outfit. And I won't be on welfare anymore."*

Jessie: *"What I would love is to be able to work. I don't want to be rich, just able to pay my bills, when my kids need something, to buy it for them."*

Irene: *"I'd like my life to be better than it is now. I'd love to see myself walking into an office and say, 'I'm working.' That would really make me feel good. Just to leave my house in the morning and just to walk into a building and just stand there and look for a few minutes, close my eyes and then open them up and say, 'Is it true?' That's what I really want."*

Dreaming the Dream

Putting it all together, several women envisioned lives in which they had it all—a home, a good job, and some personal happiness.

Amelia: *"In five years, we'll still be in this house. We will still have the cat and the dog. I'll have a brand-new car. I will be full-time employed with either JTPA or I'm going to have my own day-care center. I just hope my children are healthy and happy and they can get rid of the stress in their lives. And I sure hope I find someone as great as my dad. I really do envy my mother. She picked the number one pickle in the barrel. I think that's what she called him."*

Joy: *"In seven years I see me in my own place, in my own job, and my children in school. I hope to marry my boyfriend when I finish school. He is very nice—I lucked out with this one. He is a security guard. I'd like to finally be one big family unit—a happy family, working, and taking care of myself and my children."*

Faith: *"I want to be in good health and I want to be able to do all the things I like to do. I like to garden, wash clothes, ride my bike, and dance and sing and be with my family, and just enjoy myself. Have a job, be working."*

Arlene: *"In my future I see my job, my employment at the Central Bank to knock down roadblocks or barriers, as far as me achieving my goals and renting a farmhouse. I'm not looking for a man, but someday I really do want to get married.*

"My really big goal is to buy my own farmhouse. I really want to raise my kids the way I was raised. Maybe not that poorly, but I want them to appreciate life's simplicities. I want them to feel the peace with being in nature—the free things in life, being around animals, and just the feel of nature. It just makes you feel good."

Carol: *"I want to learn to drive. I want to see my house in one piece, finally. And I want to say 'bye-bye' to welfare and just be self-supporting. I'd like to meet somebody and fall in love. And I'd like to maintain my health and just keep going."*

These are the dreams of poor women raising children alone. They don't dream of vacations, fancy houses, fame and recognition, clothes, jewelry, or any number of luxury items for themselves. Rather, they hope for a home of their own, a decent job, an opportunity for further education, some money for their children's futures, and maybe love. Most of the women have none of these basics, except in their dreams. Some have earned academic degrees or are seeking better-paying jobs, both of which may help them to obtain some aspects of their vision for the future. Others have the dreams, but the way to achieve them is not clear. Perhaps what is most remarkable is that most of them still have dreams.

NINE. A Job Is Not Enough

How do the dreams of these women—dreams of a home, reasonable incomes, a car that runs, a future for their children—become realities? What will it take to transform lives of poverty and struggle into lives with more income and opportunities?

Several themes emerge from the stories of the thirty women. Underlying almost all of their choices and how they live their lives is that the women are *mothers first*. Their most important role is that of mother, their most important priority is the well-being of their children. They view the provider role through the lens of motherhood, not vice versa. For them, the greatest pain of poverty is how it affects their children. The major reason they keep struggling is because of their children.

Another theme is that of *I have always worked*. As girls, they baby-sat, cooked, and cleaned. As adults, they work behind assembly lines or restaurant counters and then go home to cook and clean for themselves and their children. Despite their efforts, the women still live in poverty. The third theme, that the women are *marginalized, but motivated* provides a partial explanation of their circumstances. Their minimal earnings stem from lack of opportunities, not lack of effort. They do not have the requisite education and training for better-paying jobs. Out of the mainstream, they are not aware of possibilities. Many are isolated from any form of social support. But with great effort they keep rowing their shaky boats forward.

A fourth theme is that *child care is not child raising*. The time and attention the women need to give to their children puts the relationship between child care and child raising in perspective. Finding reliable child care is necessary and important, but only one part of a parent's job. Deferring an educational opportunity to care for a sick child, tending a frightened child in the middle of the night, and making the dinner after a tiring day behind the counter or assembly line are also what being a parent is all about. It is the raising of the child, and trying to do it well, that underscores the stresses and strains of being a single mother.

Having *stone soup for supper again* speaks to the women's perseverance and ingenuity in the midst of adversity. They make do with very little money. A family bus ride and a child's own pan pizza are special treats, thanks to overtime pay. A pack of gum or books from the school book fair are denied if the money is gone before the end of the month. Feeding the child is a higher priority than one's pride if a local charity must be tapped. And sometimes it is not weeks or months, but years that the women live in such poverty.

A sixth theme is that the women have been *betrayed* by their mates and many have been *wounded* by physical violence or emotional pain. They describe the physical and emotional abuse their former mates and spouses inflicted on them and sometimes on their children. They tell of a mate's drug and alcohol addictions, and describe negative behaviors resulting from these addictions. The women describe men who disappear and fail to support their children. And they recall, sadly and with pain, that these were the men they loved, lived with, and married.

They are *women of commitment and of hardship*. They take care of their children and do not give up. They try to be a family, playing several parts at once. There is rarely anyone to help them. Public assistance is an option of necessity, not choice. They are heroines for trying to live on assistance and heroines for trying, with few resources, to make a life for themselves and their children without it.

These themes—*mothers first; I have always worked; marginalized, but motivated; child care is not child raising; stone soup for supper again; betrayed and wounded;* and *women of commitment and hardship*—capture some of the life experiences of mothers in poverty and help us to understand the women and their circumstances. These themes exist in both rural and urban environments, despite the demographic differences between them, and suggest that women's poverty is more systemic than demographic. Effective remedies need to address the issues emanating from these commonalities. The next step is to take the themes and voices that underlie them and develop a framework for action. Such a focus or plan can guide concrete actions that will improve the lives of the women and their children and help them move permanently out of poverty.

From Understanding to Action: A Framework for a Future

One purpose of this research was to look at issues pertaining to poor women and work within the context of their life histories and social circumstances. A qualitative-data-gathering strategy was used to capture the voices of the women. The purpose and approach has produced a broad and multifaceted picture of their lives. An effective action framework needs to be holistic as well. Just as the voices have given us a more complete picture of the lives of the women, so, too, the framework for action is one that encompasses several factors and recognizes that all of these forms of action need to be in place simultaneously for successful outcomes to occur.

An effective framework would encompass three components: income opportunities; social support and linking systems; and help and healing. The examination of the women's lives in context suggests that all three of these areas need to be addressed. Like a three-legged stool, all three legs are necessary to form a firm stepping stool out of poverty. The lack of one leg can topple the stool.

The first component in the framework for a future is an income opportunity. Without the opportunity to earn an income sufficient to support a family, there is no way to move beyond poverty. An income opportunity is one that provides the possibility of earning a family wage with good benefits, offers a good chance of increased earnings over time, and has possibilities for growth in skills and advancement. It is defined broadly, as there are many ways to enhance income potential. Income opportunities considered here are post-secondary education, higher-paying nontraditional jobs, interest-based training, and entrepreneurial opportunities.

The second component is a work and community support system that recognizes and facilitates the women's dual roles as mothers and providers. No matter how strong the leg of income opportunities is, the stool will tip over unless a support system addressing their many needs is in place. A broad-based social support and linking system would include information networks, communal housing and resource sharing, learning links between the women and other members of the community, and a work-family partnership perspective.

Help and healing is the aspect of the framework that has received the least amount of public attention. But the women need this component as much as the other two components. Even without the extreme brutalities of domestic violence, the psychological battering these women have lived with must be healed. The women and their families need to rebuild a solid personal foundation. Then they can successfully channel their energies and efforts into the struggle out of poverty.

All three aspects of the action framework operating in tandem can be a strong stepping stool for the women, one that can support the weight of the life histories and social circumstances that make leaving poverty so hard. As the ABC's of poverty reveal, no one factor propels the women into poverty. So, too, leaving poverty permanently requires attending to the multiple needs of securing income opportunities, having a social support and linking system, and access to help and healing.

As we move from understanding to action, the next step is to flesh out the framework. What would the specific features of each component of such a framework be? What would each component look like if filled in with concrete action-oriented ideas, programs, and plans? The remainder of this chapter presents a variety of ideas for income opportunities. Chapter 10 completes this fleshing-out process by illustrating some specific elements of a social support and linking system and presenting ways that help and healing fit into the action framework.

Income Opportunities: One Size Does Not Fit All

An income opportunity is an opportunity to earn enough money to support the economic needs of a woman and her children. It would bring a woman and her family not only above our national poverty thresholds, but significantly above minimal standards such that an emergency doesn't automatically plummet the family back into poverty. It is an opportunity for income growth, a first step toward an increasing wage to meet changing family needs, especially as the children grow up and need help with opportunities of their own, such as education.

An income opportunity is one that gives a woman a reasonable chance for fulfilling some of her dreams. Eva wants "to live comfortably"; Carla, "to have a nice home, a nice car, some money in the bank"; and Jessie, "to be able to pay my bills, when my kids need something, to buy it for them." The women would like the economic strength to have some of the basics in life for themselves and their children and the economic security such that they can maintain a reasonable quality of life for their families.

Equating income opportunity with "a job" can be a barrier to considering a wide range of income opportunities. The research outcomes indicate clearly that a job rarely provides the requisite economic foundation. Many of the women now have or have had jobs. "I have always worked," they say. But, at best, the factory and restaurant jobs keep the wolf away from the door. The jobs pay more than public assistance, although help, such as rent or heat subsidies, is usually still needed. At worst, the jobs become holding actions against extreme poverty until a crisis pushes these women back on public assistance. A job that is low-paying, that lacks advancement, and that places a woman in a marginalized, vulnerable, and powerless position in the work system is a job leading nowhere. It is not an income opportunity.

Another barrier to committing energies and funds to income opportunity possibilities is the myth that poor women are lazy and not motivated to work. The women's efforts refute the myth and highlight the reality of their being motivated, but marginalized. They lack skills, education, and training opportunities, and an awareness of possibilities. But they do not lack a strong work ethic. Just ask them. One need only spend a day with Jean, as she raises five school-age children and works part-time in a food processing plant, or with Marie, with three children and a clerical job that she's held for over seven years, to know how hard they work.

Sufficient earnings and advancement opportunities are the keys to fulfilling their dreams. But not all women can take the same route to acquiring an effective income opportunity. Circumstances, personal inclinations, and skills and abilities vary. The wider the range of opportunities available, the better the chance of matching the person's capabilities with the opportunity's requirements, thereby increasing the probability of success.

Post-Secondary Education

Education has always been the cornerstone of enhanced employment opportunities. A college degree can provide access to many income opportunities, such as professional, technical, managerial, and administrative positions not accessible to high school graduates. Cathy Henderson and Cecilia Ottinger (1986), for example, found that women college graduates surpassed the average earnings of their cohorts who had only a high school degree within two years of graduation. While a high school degree or a GED is an essential first step toward economic independence, it cannot always be viewed as an ending, at least not for women trying to support families on their earnings.

The experiences of the women in the study offer solid evidence that it is possible to pursue post-secondary education successfully, even for those resuming school at the tenth- or eleventh-grade levels. Both Gloria and Pat were high school dropouts. While raising their children as single mothers, they managed to complete their GEDs and then go on to obtain associate degrees. Recall Gloria's pride in her 3.8 average. Julie and Arlene also obtained associate college degrees while raising young children alone. Job opportunities and expectations are greatly expanded for these women. Arlene's new job has a respectable starting salary, provides very good benefits, and has clear opportunities for advancement. Julie and Gloria speak of going on to finish college. Pat dreams of returning to college for a law degree.

Efforts to provide and expand post-secondary educational opportunities for poor single mothers can have big payoffs. Gender and race discrimination notwithstanding, as college graduates these women will have a far easier time finding jobs that pay a family wage and offer advancement opportunities than those without such degrees. Moreover, by bringing an educational and skill base to their jobs, they are in a stronger position from which to negotiate permanent or occasional working arrangements that mesh with parenting needs. With jobs that pay well, the price for being a mother first can be far less than with low-paying jobs in which employees are more replaceable than valued. Finally, again as evidenced by the women in the study, the increase in self-esteem, personal pride, and dignity, and role modeling for their own children also make it a worthwhile investment.

Notably, discussions of opportunities for poor single mothers to get a college degree are not a significant part of our public debate, if such discussions are held at all. The negative stereotype of the lazy and unmotivated poor mother, especially the single mother on public assistance, suggests that they cannot or will not pursue post-secondary education. But the voices of many of the poor women tell us otherwise. Recall the efforts and perseverance of the four women who returned to school. As Julie described her graduation, "It was like fireworks and cotton candy and the whole nine yards."

Indeed, the option of post-secondary education is such a good one in terms of return on investment to the women, their children, and to society, that one wonders why it has received so little attention. Our efforts to keep the poor at a distance, to see them as different, to look for scapegoats, or to maintain traditional gender roles may be blinding us to workable solutions to the problems of poverty among single mothers. Perhaps the intractable problem is not how to improve the lives of poor single mothers, but rather how to change society's views about them so that opportunities with high payoffs can be in the forefront of consideration, not on the back burner.

Nontraditional Job Opportunities

Although a college degree offers the opportunity to earn far more than minimum wage, it is not for everyone. Another income opportunity for the women lies in training for and entering the higher paying, more male-dominated skill and craft jobs. Jobs in the areas of carpentry, electronics, plumbing, construction, industrial maintenance, and transportation pay three and four times more than deadend, minimum-wage jobs. These are traditionally held by men, who are able to earn incomes matching the needs of their role as the breadwinner. These jobs, with their higher wages, are just as appropriate and necessary for women who are breadwinners.

According to Brigid O'Farrell and Suzanne Moore (1993), data collected from 1979 to 1989 show that women can enter and remain in blue-collar jobs historically done by men, even under difficult circumstances. The pay is good and the women are satisfied with their pay and with the work itself. In a study of women in skilled and semiskilled jobs, such as machinists, pipe fitters, and telephone repairers, the average income was $30,000 per year, significantly higher than most traditionally female occupations (Kissman 1990). Mary

Walshok (1981), in a pioneering study of women in nontraditional jobs, found high levels of job satisfaction, and the women described their jobs as complex, interesting, and challenging. And Janina Latack, Bonnie Roach, Sasen Josephs, and Mitchell Levine (1987), looking at participants in a three- to four-year carpentry apprenticeship program, found, based on performance and satisfaction, that the transition into carpentry is as successful for women as for men.

Although there is high resistance to women in blue-collar jobs and some of these jobs are increasingly susceptible to attrition from technological changes and shifts in the economy, O'Farrell and Moore (1993) conclude that women need to focus on blue-collar jobs because of the high wages. The job growth is modest, but positive. A shortage of workers is projected in some skilled jobs, particularly newly developing semiskilled and skilled occupations. Traditional blue-collar trades, such as construction and machining, continue to provide job opportunities for women and men.

Step Up, a pilot project in Chicago, demonstrates the feasibility of training welfare mothers in housing renovation skills, such as plumbing and plastering (Wilkerson 1994). With the cooperation of local trade unions, the Chicago Housing Authority hires and trains people to renovate and repair vacant public housing. The jobs are for eighteen months and pay $13.52 per hour. In the short term, the women are off of welfare and earning a good family wage. In the long run they are being trained for a variety of nontraditional jobs available in the private or public sector. Of the first group of 298 participants, 115 dropped out or were dismissed, and 2 died; 131 are still in the training program and 18 of these are in a longer carpentry apprenticeship program, and 50 have graduated and are in other construction jobs earning about $19 per hour. Given that there are thousands of abandoned public housing units in the country and three billion dollars in rehabilitation money available to pay for the work to get done, programs like Step Up could supply women with the skills they need to find jobs in higher-paying nontraditional fields.

The 1991 passage of the Nontraditional Employment Act for Women also offers promise for training for low-income women in nontraditional jobs. The act encourages the Job Training and Partnership Act (JTPA) Private Industry Councils (PICs) to set goals for training women participants in nontraditional (and higher-paying) jobs. The outcomes thus far of Wider Opportunities for Women's nontraditional training programs within JTPA illustrate the value and viability of such training (Wider Opportunities for

Women, Inc., 1993). For example, in rural Montana twenty-four of the thirty women who have completed training now work in the Departments of Transportation and Forestry or for private contractors. Some are earning up to $20 per hour. In Milwaukee women are being trained as machinists, welders, carpenters, and printers, putting them on career paths toward annual salaries over $30,000 (Coleman 1993). Potential for nontraditional training is also found in the Intermodal Surface Transportation Efficiency Act of 1991. The act, which provides money to states for highways, bridges, and alternative forms of transportation, gives states the option of putting substantial funds into the recruitment and training of women and minorities for construction employment.

A key step is to promote awareness of and encourage access to nontraditional positions. Only two women in this study, LaVerne and Eva, had held nontraditional jobs. As a group, the range of knowledge of occupations open to the women was not only limited to traditional female occupations, such as nurse and beautician, but limited even within this range. Yet the interest and abilities reflected in Marilyn's description of work in the foundry or Carol's home repair and renovation saga, as well as the perseverance shown by so many of the women, suggest that investment in this area would also have a high payoff.

Interest-based Training

Another income opportunity for the women is through training that can lead to higher-paying jobs in their expressed areas of interest. Many women spoke of interests and abilities in cooking, cleaning, restaurant work, taking care of others, and working with people. Yet few saw links between these interests and a livable wage. They were not steered toward nor did they have any models who might demonstrate the possible livelihoods in these areas.

If we just took a sampling of interests and projected them onto positions that pay well, a host of income opportunities would emerge. Interest in foods and cooking could lead to being a restaurant chef, nutritional consultant, or dietary researcher. Hotel and restaurant management is a vast field, with many positions reflective of the kinds of interests expressed by these women. Care of the elderly is a growing field and one that many of the women were genuinely excited about. Well-paying positions with opportunities for advancement are also increasing in health-care fields.

With few role models, and social and work role expectations based on traditional gender roles, the women lack awareness and knowledge of many viable work opportunities and possibilities. There is no one who might encourage and direct them to look beyond "a job" to technical and professional positions in occupations. The women are motivated, but have been marginalized from mainstream opportunities. This was true regardless of where the women live. Despite views of corporate office towers, the women in the large city were just as marginalized and isolated as those with geographical distances separating them from employment opportunities.

Vicki, with two young children, spoke excitedly about her interest in the elderly. Severely allergic to a chemical used in nursing home cleaning, she is now unemployed and is looking for factory work. With the appropriate intervention, she could be on her way to a career in some form of elder care, which sparks her interest and enthusiasm. Her ability to work a double shift in the nursing home indicates her motivation, energy, and stamina. She has the makings of success. But if she remains marginalized and isolated, she may drift on and off of public assistance.

Emily, with four young children, is also stuck. When talking with me, she commented on two single mothers, one going into nursing and one into computers. She felt she should pursue work in one of these two fields, although she had neither the interest nor the ability to do so. She displayed much artistic talent and had schooling in art. These artistic talents emerged in her work and activities with her children. But she saw only two provider routes out of public assistance. It's no wonder she feels stuck and defeated. If she could widen her horizons and link her artistic interests with an occupation, she would be able to take more direct steps toward economic self-sufficiency.

These women have a wide range of talents and interests, and the motivation and perseverance to pursue good opportunities. The excitement and motivation of those in caretaking positions illustrates the motivation. Nancy is well on her way to becoming an occupational therapist. Susan, as a nurse's aide, is deciding between becoming a licensed practical nurse or registered nurse. Both women love their fields and see future opportunities for themselves in these fields. A perceived link by other women between interest and opportunity could generate the same excitement for those with other interests. We need to tap more into the women's motivation and interests by expanding their own career knowledge and expectations and widening the range and quality of opportunities available to them.

Entrepreneurship

During the past twenty years, there has been a remarkable rise in the number of small businesses owned and operated by women. In 1976 only 4.6 percent of all small businesses were owned by women. In 1987 that number jumped to 30 percent and Labor Department officials estimate that it could reach 50 percent by the year 2000 (Nelton 1989). Many professional women, after hitting their heads on the corporate glass ceiling, have turned to starting such enterprises. For those with children, it has proven to be a good way to combine work and family.

Similarly, starting and running a small-business venture could be a good income opportunity for poor single mothers facing the cellar ceiling barrier and the mother-provider balancing dilemma. The American Women's Economic Development Corporation in New York City offered three cycles of a forty-two-week course in entrepreneurship and small-business management to a total of seventy-six unemployed and low-income women. The New Directions course, cosponsored by the City of New York and several corporate donors through 1994, was free to the participants, who learned about business plans, sale and contract negotiation, advertising and public relations, and accounting and product development. Their new-venture ideas included a cleaning service, video production, jewelry manufacturing, floral arranging, and real estate management.

An evaluation of a small self-employment demonstration project (Rabin and Moore 1991) showed that efforts in this area can be an effective way for poor women to leave welfare and move toward economic independence and growth. In three separate sites in Pennsylvania, business training and assistance in finding funding for microbusinesses were provided to welfare recipients, primarily women, recruited into the demonstration program. At the end of the program, thirty-two of sixty-four welfare clients (50 percent) started a business or obtained employment, whereas, at best, 27 percent of a statewide comparison group went off welfare during the time periods of the demonstration project. The program participants overwhelmingly stated that the business training had helped them achieve their goals by increasing their self-confidence and providing them with the skills and information to start a business and do a business plan.

On a larger scale, the Women's Economic Development Corporation (WEDCO) in Minnesota offers comprehensive services to women engaged in small-business operations. In its first three years (1984–87), it assisted over two thousand women, 75 percent with incomes under $15,000 and 45 percent with incomes under $7,000. WEDCO also offers access to financing through conventional lenders or through its own funds. Business ventures of WEDCO clients include: snow plowing, upholstering, manufacturing fishing lures, and teaching dance (Gould, Stern, and Lyman 1989).

Successful approaches to assisting low-income women in entrepreneurial efforts can be found in models developed for financing such ventures among poor women in third world and developing countries. Once such model is that employed by the Foundation for International Community Assistance, which currently assists over 511 groups of poor women in Mexico and seven other Latin American countries (Carstens 1991). Underlying their successful lending approach is the formation of the women into "village banks" or income-generating groups. These groups offer their members a series of short-term loans for income-generating projects. The women manage their own income-generating groups, which gives them experience in making their own decisions and the opportunity to learn to create options for themselves and their communities. Repayment rates in most national programs range from 100 percent to 95 percent.

Consideration of such models can spark new ideas for assisting the poor. For example, a small pilot project based on microenterprise development models used with third world countries is being tried out in Baltimore (Friedman 1994). The project is intended to show how microentrepreneurs, such as a mother who does hair styling out of her home, can grow with a small loan and business plan.

There are high risks and many pitfalls in new venture start-ups, especially in the early stages. Roberta Spalter-Roth, Enrique Soto, and Lily Zandniapour's (1994) research, for example, points up the value of additional financial and social supports to supplement self-employment income. Nonetheless, the entrepreneurship route can lead to a good income opportunity for those women with the interest, talent, and inclination for such ventures. Renata dreamed of owning her own restaurant and Amelia was interested in starting her own day-care center. Pat, a paralegal, spoke of starting a legal services office with evening and Saturday hours for working mothers. Jessie used to have a furniture refinishing business, as she wanted to work out of her home to be close to her children. For women living in rural areas, businesses run out of the home could provide the income opportunities not available in their locale. For many women, training opportunities and financing assistance to start a business might well pay off in future independence and reasonable incomes.

At the Macro Level

The focus here is on the individual level, looking at ways the women can gain access to income opportunities. It is important to place the discussion, albeit briefly, within the context of macro forces that can help or hinder their efforts. Changes in organizational, educational, and societal arenas can facilitate the efforts of the women to enhance their income opportunities.

Providing ways for women to move out of low-level, low-paying jobs is the key to their improved futures. At the organizational level, efforts can also be made to raise the wages, expand benefits, and improve the conditions of these jobs so that they offer the financial independence and dignity they now lack. Cooperative Home Care, for example, is an organization that is seeking to improve conditions and promote careers in the home health care industry, which traditionally pays its part-time workforce only slightly more than the minimum wage of $4.25, with no benefits. Cooperative Home Care offers training, higher wages, medical, dental, and vacation benefits and a guarantee of at least thirty hours of work a week. In addition, the company is organized as a for-profit enterprise to enable employee ownership and profit sharing (Martin 1994). This and similar models being started around the country, with private foundation backing, illustrate how changes at the organizational and industry level can contribute to the enhancement of income opportunities for poor single mothers.

Also at the macro level, the elimination of gender and race discrimination in the workplace and the classroom will play an important role in enhancing income opportunities for impoverished single mothers. The efforts of the women have been constrained by unequal treatment of women and people of color. Nontraditional jobs may pay more, but as the Weidman, White, and Swartz (1988) study of an electronic technician program showed, sexual harassment in male-dominated fields has not disappeared. The women in the program were subjected to racially and sexually prejudicial remarks from other students and faculty.

The fight for equality of opportunity is ongoing. Although there have been great strides forward since the passage of the Civil Rights Act in 1964, the struggle continues. Despite significant efforts to promote equality of opportunity, bias against women and minorities still exists in training, hiring, promotion, and loan-financing decisions. Bias appears in the wage differentials and occupational segregation that contribute to women's lower earning power. While developing income opportunities for the women, it is important to continue efforts to reduce and eliminate racial and gender discrimination in the employment sector. Reducing these macro-level barriers, through legislative action as well as general societal changes, will promote equality of opportunity for all women and people of color in the workplace and, therefore, will contribute to enhancing income opportunities for poor single mothers.

Similarly, educational systems still foster gender stereotypes and traditional gender roles for women. For example, there has been little change in sex-segregated enrollment patterns in vocational education: boys are more likely to be enrolled in programs leading to higher-paying jobs (Wirt, et al. 1989). According to a report of the American Association of University Women (1992), girls continue to confront barriers to equal participation in school and society. And minority girls and girls from low-income families face particularly severe obstacles. More than likely the women in this study experienced these barriers when they were young. Their own aspirations were not bolstered by the educational system nor were they helped with setting productive goals for the future. Changes here will also contribute to the total effort. In all of these arenas—organizational, educational, and societal—efforts toward macro-level change complement and contribute to the individual efforts of the women to improve their lives.

A Job Is Not Enough

Using the term income opportunity takes us beyond that of "getting a job" to seeking sources and opportunities that can provide a good income for the family. Only a good income will move single mothers out of poverty permanently. Income opportunities reflect a positive perspective, one that opens up creative and wide-ranging thinking with regard to opportunities for the women.

The women have always worked, but lacking skills and education, have not gotten very far. They are motivated, but are marginalized and have limited access to the resources necessary to gain access to mainstream opportunities. Developing broad-based income opportunities, such as postsecondary education, nontraditional job opportunities, interest-based training, and entrepreneurial ventures, will move the women out of the margins and into the mainstream. Creative approaches to employment counseling and increasing the women's awareness of and accessibility to these income opportunities are important complements to these endeavors, as are changes at the macro level. All of these are efforts of hope and commitment to the futures of these women and their children.

TEN. A Community of Efforts

With the three-legged stool to support their efforts, poor single mothers
have a chance to improve the quality of life for themselves and their
families. Without it, many women will remain stuck. Others will valiantly
pursue income opportunities, struggle with the multiple demands and strains,
and fall back into poverty, disillusioned and blaming themselves for their
failures.

The remaining legs of the stepping stool out of poverty are a social support
and linking system and opportunities for help and healing. The need for these
two components is woven throughout the preceding chapters. The women's
stresses, fatigue, demanding work-school-family schedules, and isolated and
marginalized lives all speak to the significant role that both social support and
help/healing play in overcoming the barriers to leaving poverty. These
components of the framework for a future will facilitate and enhance the

efforts of the women as they strive to improve their circumstances and deal with difficult life situations.

A Social Support and Linking System

The second component of a framework for a future is a social support and linking system that addresses the women's need for multiple supports. A support system responsive to the realities of their lives might include information networks, communal housing and resource sharing, learning links, and the implementation of a work-family partnership perspective.

The difficulties and complexities of their life situations call for a broad and multifaceted view of support needs. An effective social support and linking system is one that goes well beyond a narrow range of options, such as focusing primarily on child-care arrangements for the working single mother. There is no question that child care is essential for the working single mother. Quality day care and subsidies for low-income women are critical needs. But just as "a job" is an inadequate income opportunity, so, too, "a job sprinkled with a little day care" is a limited view of support requirements.

A "work-plus-day-care-equals-success" equation implies that adding day care to the equation balances things out for the working mother and that she can now assume the role of traditional breadwinner. But it is not reflective of nor does it incorporate the requirements and demands of motherhood. Child care is not child raising, and the responsibilities of mothering are not offset just by adding day care to the equation. These women are mothers first, and that role is their first priority. They need support as mothers, as providers, and for the balancing these roles require. If it takes a village to raise a child, then it takes a community of efforts to support the women as they move themselves and their children out of poverty.

Information Networks

Efforts to encourage and provide the opportunity for sharing information and experiences among poor single mothers are essential parts of a social-support system. Most of the women in the study had limited information as to what opportunities were available to them. Julie, for example, stumbled on the WT Program in her area through a job training office listing in the blue pages of the telephone book. Anita believed there would be help for her as a single mother when she was ready to learn about computers, but she had no idea where to go for such information. There were large variations in the women's knowledge of available assistance and opportunities. Operating alone and without much help, most stumbled onto opportunities through trial and error.

National, state, and local level networks linking women with each other for information-sharing and support would ensure that most, rather than only a few, women would be aware of opportunities and programs already in place. With such a network, the women could share experiences, recount what worked and didn't work, and pass on helpful information. The network could provide knowledge about where to go for certain types of training, ensuring that all the women are aware of all possible income opportunities, as well as support services. Through information-sharing and network-building, some women might also see opportunities to pool their resources and enter into entrepreneurial ventures.

The networks, by providing opportunities for experience-sharing, can become a source of much-needed social support and encouragement. Sharing experiences reduces isolation and enhances self-esteem. In addition, by sharing ideas and experiences the women learn to help each other. As an example, the women who went through the WT Programs saw themselves as part of a group. Susan described herself as a "WT girl" and Julie said "we" and "women like us" many times in our conversation. The positive sentiment toward the WT group suggests that it could easily be converted to a weekly or bimonthly program, providing the women with ongoing social support at the local level.

Finally, information and support networks may help ease the transition from public assistance to full-time employment. Carol, Marie, and, to some extent, Julie all expressed concerns about the additional costs, especially for child care and health care benefits, that they might incur in their transition to full-time employment. Their concerns add to and reinforce the calls for national policies providing affordable health care and child care (Sidell 1986; Polakow 1993, among others). Such policies would greatly facilitate the transition process. In addition, women who have made successful transitions and those, like Julie, with specific information about what the system will or will not provide, can be valuable resources to those in the transition phase.

Community Living and Resource Sharing

The idea of a community of efforts could be extended beyond experience and information sharing to more structured community living and resource-sharing arrangements. The women I spoke with all had special skills and abilities that could complement those of other women. If such skills, talents, and energies could be pooled, many more women might be able to leave poverty permanently.

Community housing for single mothers would facilitate resource sharing and meet the need for affordable housing, an important issue for many of the women. Not only would costs be shared and therefore lowered, but the daily responsibilities of household and children would be shared and lightened as well. Communal housing arrangements say clearly that child care is not child raising. Such arrangements could provide many of the supports and emergency backups that a struggling single mother needs.

The Women's Housing Coalition, Inc., in Albuquerque, New Mexico, offers low-income and homeless women with children affordable housing; training in basic property management and support services, such as job readiness, job placement, and self-development; and referrals to other community resources. Most recently the Women's Housing Coalition celebrated the success of several former clients on their way to moving out of poverty—two college graduates, nine women in school full-time, and four with full-time jobs. A similar form of transitional community housing is Warren Village, founded by the Warren United Methodist Church in Denver, Colorado (*New York Times* 1988). Warren Village offers subsidized apartments, day care, counseling, support groups, and evening classes to approximately ninety single-parent families.

Another form of resource trading through housing is being experimented with by Bethel New Life in Chicago (Pendleton 1990). It is building fifty new homes in impoverished West Garfield Park. Half of these three-bedroom town houses will be occupied by women providing day care so that the other mothers in the neighborhood can go to work. Mothers in all three of these communal housing enterprises speak of the sense of self-confidence and hope for their children's future that these opportunities and surroundings give them. Extensions of these models, as a shared living community, might include pooled transportation to work or school sites, ongoing information- and experience-sharing groups, literacy programs, training opportunities brought to the community, and self- and educational-enhancement programs designed by the women in the community.

Efforts to encourage and promote resource trading can be of particular help to those women for whom working out of the home is not possible. Through forms of resource sharing, a woman with a health problem or a child with a serious health problem can contribute to the community and be reimbursed for her efforts. The women running the day-care centers are good examples of how this can work to everyone's advantage. Moreover, even if her resource contribution still requires some help from public assistance, she is no longer isolated and need not suffer a sense of failure.

Ursula had to stay home with her epileptic daughter. During those years she volunteered in her daughter's school, moving eventually into the role of girls' basketball coach. Despite her obvious contributions to others, she felt and still feels "low rated" about being on public assistance. A resource-sharing support system would give value and meaning to the efforts of women like Ursula.

Both the information networks and the larger-scale communal efforts can be major forces for change in the women's lives. For single mothers with limited job skills, going it alone, no matter how great the effort, can be more frustrating than fruitful. As LaVerne said, "I don't know why life should be so hard. I get on a boat and I get going and something happens and I fall back again. It seems like I never get anywhere but I work real hard." Aided by a community of efforts, LaVerne could finally get somewhere.

Learning Links

A third aspect of a broadly designed support system is links between the women and members of the community at large, especially other women. Three such linkages are mothering role models, work and school mentors, and advising roles. These links can help the women to learn from others as well as bring them out of the margins and into the mainstream.

Some of the women had very good mothers upon whom to model their own mothering behaviors. Others were not so fortunate. Julie, now the mother of two children, said that she knew nothing about life skills and she valued lessons in nutrition, dress, and "things other people take for granted." It might be useful to forge a learning link between women like Julie, and women and men in the community who have raised children, are confident in their parenting skills, and would like to pass on this knowledge. Women who invested their "career years" in child raising, grandparents far from their families, and the elderly without partners come to mind as both model teachers and people who could also gain and grow from such an experience.

College education, nontraditional jobs, and, in general, work beyond that of minimum-wage jobs are new experiences for most of the women. Helpful here are learning links with women who are engaged in these income-opportunity experiences. As one-on-one mentors they could provide support and offer advice. If the mentors were mothers as well, they could guide the women as they learn to develop a mother-provider balance that works for them.

Both types of learning links pull the women out of the margins and into the mainstream. Mentoring and modeling are powerful learning techniques, ones taken for granted by those in the mainstream. These learning links can provide the women with guides to point out the holes and rough spots on the road out of poverty, as well as offer opportunities for support and friendship. Moreover, there is an opportunity for women participating as models and mentors to recognize commonalities among women of all economic levels. Gender discrimination, for example, affects *all* women. Putting efforts into a job and then hitting one's head against a ceiling, whether it is the glass ceiling or the cellar ceiling, still hurts.

A third learning link is between junior-high-school age girls and the single mothers moving out of poverty. In my conversations with the women, several wanted to tell girls how to avoid their own situations. For example, Gloria wanted to tell young girls, "Get your own skills. That way you are not dependent on a husband or boyfriend. If it doesn't work out, you can make it on your own." Joy said she would like to tell girls in high school, "Don't get pregnant. Stay in school first. Watch the men. Even if the teachers don't seem very good, stay in school. You are the one that is going to get the diploma. Everyone thinks of cute smiling babies. It is not like that at all. It's hard, really hard now to have kids and be going for a GED."

These words of advice, spoken with the intensity of those who lived through the pain and struggles, could have a powerful impact on the many young women who think "it won't happen to me." In addition, participation in such a learning links program could enhance the women's own sense of self-esteem and self-worth, which has usually been badly damaged by their negative experiences. By helping others through the sharing of their own life experiences and lessons learned, they would be helped as well.

A Work-Family Partnership Perspective

Finally, a viable support system must include a realistic and workable consideration of the child-care needs of a single working mother. To accomplish this, the work-family issue needs to have more of a partnership perspective, one that includes the responsibilities of employers, unions, child-care providers, and the community in facilitating the mother-provider role. At present, most of the responsibility is placed on the women needing the child-care services. A partnership perspective redistributes this responsibility among those employing parents, those representing the parents in the workplace, child-care providers, and the working parent. All need to see themselves as participants in this partnership.

While many companies are improving their work-family support efforts, it is often the low-paying positions that provide little flexibility for the working parent. As the research revealed, these are the positions most commonly held by the women. Recall Jean's company, a food-processing plant, that abruptly changed her starting time from 7 AM to 6 AM, leaving her with a one-hour gap before the day-care center opened. LaVerne, working on the assembly line in a dog-bone factory, had to take her sick child to the doctors frequently. She was fired for missing work. Julie was asked to come to a late-night work meeting at the supermarket. Unable to find a sitter, she quit her job rather than take her asthmatic daughter out in the cold weather.

Elizabeth Mulroy and Marcy Pitt-Catsouphes (1994) found that single parents in the workplace experience greater anxiety, more career setbacks, and a sense of being viewed by bosses with mistrust. Single parents, in this case single mothers, should not be punished for attending to their children's needs. Rather, we need to encourage and provide incentives for all employers to develop "parent-friendly" work environments. Such environments would recognize that emergencies, illnesses, and other needs of children are responsibilities to which employees must attend. A parent-friendly work environment would offer the flexibility and support that help working parents, especially the single parent, to meet family demands. Within a partnership perspective, both the employer and employee work together to assess and resolve work-family conflicts.

Unions can play an active role in this partnership as well. Over the last fifteen years unions have increased their work-family policy efforts and focus. Susan Cowell (1993) suggests that unions can be a better force than corporate America in this area. Labor has always argued that adequate income to support a family, primarily through good, secure jobs, is the most basic of all family needs. Unionization raises women's wages (Amott 1993). The corporate agenda on family excludes issues of income and job security and, according to Cowell, encourages the creation and sustenance of a low-wage workforce. As she argues, "whatever its limitations, the labor movement is . . . the best vehicle for creating a society that accommodates the needs of work and family, a society that provides equality for women and security and opportunity for all" (p. 129).

Flexibility is an important consideration for child-care providers who serve mothers with unusual or variable work schedules. Many nontraditional income opportunities, such as blue-collar jobs or small-business opportunities, require nontraditional hours as well. As an example of such flexibility, one child-care center set up operations in a trailer at a construction site. It allowed the women workers flexibility in hours and access to their children. Moreover, when the construction job moved to another site, the child-care center trailer moved with it.

The impoverished single mother also needs child-care assistance during nonwork hours. Recall Carla, who had to quit her GED studies. Although she had someone to take care of her young children during work hours, the after-work responsibilities and demands she faced left her with no time or energy to study for the GED. Mothers like Carla could use "respite centers," places where the mothers can safely and comfortably take their children for an hour, an evening, or even a day so they can recoup, recover, or catch up with all their chores and responsibilities. Community centers and YWCAs, for example, offer hourly child care, although usually for a fee. In some locations, the Children's Aid Society provides a respite center, including overnight stays for children in families undergoing severe stress. With these ongoing services as models, nonprofit community groups might offer similar services to poor single mothers and become part of the work-family partnership.

With a partnership perspective, the responsibility of child care for single mothers is spread among all concerned. Job demands that go outside of the usual working hours, travel requirements, caring for a sick child, and child-care needs during work and non-work hours all become something to "work out" among the partnership members. It is a holistic approach to work and family. The partnership perspective recognizes the kinks and wrinkles and smoothes them out by spreading them out. The single working mother is no longer alone.

Help and Healing

Many impoverished women have experienced negative life situations, especially in the relationships with their mates. They struggle with the stresses of poverty on top of old wounds still in need of healing. To facilitate the climb out of poverty, the third leg of the stepping stool, opportunities for help and healing, needs to be in place as well.

The Toll of Domestic Violence

Dealing with and recovering from domestic violence requires help and counseling. More than one-third of the women in this study described incidents of abuse, and in several cases the incidents were severe and life threatening. According to a report by the American Psychological Association (APA) (Koss et al. 1994), as many as four million women experience severe or life-threatening assaults from a male partner in an average twelve-month period. Moreover, the report observes that minority women and women living in poverty are especially vulnerable to all forms of violence.

Domestic violence exacts a severe physical and psychological toll. Recovering from these traumatic experiences and repairing the self-esteem and sense of self-worth typically damaged in such situations usually requires counseling or other forms of supportive intervention (Walker 1984, among others). Yet few of the women received any help. Most of the women left the abusive situations and "got on" with their lives. Recall Carol, who at seventeen, with a seven-month-old baby, left her husband. "He was a wife beater. There was no one to talk to about it. I just dealt with it until I wasn't going to deal with it anymore." Or LaVerne's reaction, "He beat me three times and I was out of there." Rather than just going it alone, the women would have benefited from some form of counseling.

A few women received help during their stay in a battered women's shelter. Gloria, whose husband physically abused her and sexually assaulted their daughters, found the counseling in the shelter very helpful. Only one of the abused women, Emily, spoke of being in counseling after leaving the shelter. She, too, found it helpful, but had to stop when her money ran out. Poor women's use of mental health and related services is limited by its cost, transportation, and child care (McGrath et al. 1990).

Psychological help for families experiencing abuse is also important. The toll on the children of battered women can be high, affecting their emotional and social development (Jaffe, Wolfe, and Wilson 1990; Bray 1994). Both of Amelia's young children watched as her husband beat her. Her daughter now sleeps with the windows locked and is afraid to hand in her homework. Recall Amelia's pain as she tried to help her daughter deal with the emotional wounds of abuse.

The mothers work hard to help their children, often neglecting their own recovery to do so. Mental health professionals can play a significant role in helping these families heal from the effects of observing, living with, and experiencing violence in the home. With such interventions, both the mother and her children will be better able to grapple with the other difficult aspects of their lives.

The Shelter as a Start Up, Not a Step Down

For several women in the study, leaving the abusive relationship was the precursor to poverty. Dale MacKenzie (1985) and others have found that due to lack of skills, unavailability of jobs, or needs of the children, welfare is the only alternative for these women. They also found that husbands of battered wives typically control the finances, again making poverty and public assistance the only recourse when a wife leaves.

Escaping to a shelter for battered women need not be the first stop on the road into poverty. If more resources could be put into expanding their services, a shelter could be the first stop on the road to economic and personal independence. The 1994 APA report recommends tripling existing levels of funding for battered women's shelters. Shelters can offer information and resource-sharing about job and educational opportunities, provide life- and coping-skills assistance, and give job-search and skills-training instruction. For example, the Bloomsburg Women's Center in Pennsylvania runs a ten-week course for low-income single mothers, almost all of whom have a history of abuse. The program includes life-coping skills, job search and job readiness, motivation and confidence building and support. They are also able to provide similar counseling to women living in their shelter, as well as more basic "pre-pre" employment help to the shelter residents.

Most stays in a battered women's shelter are of a short-term nature. Many women need more time and ongoing support in order to go forward. Without it, they can fall back into greater poverty, or they return to the abusive relationship as their only economic recourse. Emily's short-term stay at a shelter allowed her and her children to escape from her abusive husband. But, as she said, "What would be really good is to have long-term shelters for women where you could just stay and stay and get job help."

If there was an opportunity to move from the shelter directly into longer-term transitional housing, more women might be able to escape poverty as well as their abuser. Access to transitional housing helped Jean, who had no job skills and had five school-age children. After her shelter stay, she was able to get a year's stay in housing facilities connected to the shelter. During that year, with ongoing support and direction from the shelter counselors, she was able to obtain her GED, take a computer course, and find a temporary job to hone her newly learned skills. After that year, she and her children moved into a subsidized apartment. As she said, "I have to give the shelter credit for getting me back on my feet. They gave me the self-confidence and the motivation I needed to get out there and get on my own."

The women enter the shelter hurt and confused. Shelters that can provide a clear direction and concrete help improve their chances for a start up, rather than a fall back into poverty. These chances could be improved even more if the next step could be to transitional housing, such as the Women's Housing Coalition, and a third step to permanent housing designed for single mothers. The tragedy of domestic violence could be turned into an opportunity for independence and a full life for the woman and her children.

Bolstering Self-Efficacy

Whether or not severe traumas have occurred, a variety of counseling and support efforts focusing on self-esteem and self-efficacy can shore up a psychological foundation weakened by past and ongoing negative and stressful experiences. Several of the women in the study grew up in families that fostered attitudes of unworthiness. Julie was told, "being you are a woman, you are dumb. You have no rights. You are no good." Susan's mother always told her "you will never be nothing," and Leona's family said she was "dumb, stupid, and ignorant." Help in dealing with the effects of these attitudes can enhance the women's motivation, aspirations and risk taking, and increase their chances for successfully carrying out their plans for leaving poverty.

Studies of several different types of short-term helping programs for disadvantaged single mothers show positive outcomes. For example, a ten-week experimental stress management program for low-income mothers resulted in improvements in feelings of psychological distress, depression, anxiety, inadequacy, self-confidence, and ego strength (Tableman et al. 1982). Evaluations of a life-skills training program (Whittington 1986), a competency-based program (Resnick 1984), and a counseling program (Knive-Ingraham 1985) also found positive changes in the women's self-esteem, coping skills, and self-confidence.

Belle (1982) and Worell (1988) caution that therapeutic strategies that only address a woman's particular conflicts can further victimize her, unless they are placed in the larger context of her poverty and societal oppression. To this end, Stanley Messer and Paul Lehrer (1976) suggest that a job-training program may be the most effective setting for the beginning of mental health treatments for low-income people because it provides a context in which they can develop realistic hope for an improved future. Conversely, the bolstering of self-esteem during training may facilitate successful outcomes. Julie, who recently completed her associate college degree, credits the support of the WT counselors for helping her through the program and elevating her sense of self-efficacy. As she says, "I'm going from a person that has been browbeaten all of her life to somebody that is emerging out of her shell."

Help and healing efforts are an important and necessary complement to the other components of the action framework. They build a solid personal foundation and strengthen the women's ability to move onto and continue on their paths out of poverty. The voices of the women attest to the toll of domestic violence on themselves and their children. These psychological wounds need healing. More employment and housing supports linked to abuse shelters can prevent downslides into poverty and provide lifts out. Bolstering self-efficacy and self-esteem increases the energies available for the permanent move out of poverty.

A Community of Efforts

One theme that underlies these two components is interdependence—individuals and groups teaching and learning, helping and sharing across income brackets and differing worlds of experience. A single mother—without money, mate, employment opportunities that pay a family wage, and managing difficult life circumstances—cannot climb out of poverty with all of these burdens on her back. To the extent we can acknowledge these burdens and the impossibility of doing it all alone, we can reduce them all by spreading them out. Within a community of efforts, the women can be empowered to find their own paths out of poverty and have a reasonable chance of success at these efforts.

Stepping out of poverty requires a base built on income opportunities, a social support and linking system, and help and healing. Each leg of the stool has many parts, reflecting the differing experiences, needs, and interests of the women. All three components contribute to a woman's successful permanent climb out of poverty. Working together, each can add to the value of the other. Income opportunities have a greater chance of success with a strong support system in place. A social support and linking system might be most beneficial after help and healing. Help and healing can provide the impetus to seek expanded income opportunities. Each one is necessary and, operating in tandem, they can help many women move out of poverty permanently. With all three of the components of a framework for a future in place, the women might, indeed, have a future. They could turn their dreams of a home, a reasonable income, a car that runs, and opportunities for their children into realities.

ELEVEN. The Broad Perspective Revisited

The broad perspective reframes the issue of women parenting in poverty, expanding it from a narrow look at welfare reform to a wider view of poverty reduction. In doing so, it poses a set of questions designed to achieve this objective. These questions include: Who are the poor single mothers? What circumstances bring them to poverty? How do they live and raise their children? What is needed to help poor single mothers move out of poverty and into lives with opportunities for themselves and their children?

My research, by addressing questions emanating from the broad perspective, provides the foundation for a framework for action designed to improve the quality of the lives of poor single mothers and their children and enhance their possibilities for the future. This action framework encompasses income opportunities, a social support and linking system, and help and healing. Out of the broad perspective comes a multifaceted approach to change. Only such a broad plan can address the complex factors underlying poverty among women raising children alone.

A Call to Action

The research findings are congruent with those of previous and concurrent studies. Spalter-Roth, Hartmann, and Andrews (1990), Zill et al. (1991), and a U.S. General Accounting Office Report (1991) point to the difficulties women have in earning a family wage and their vulnerability in the workplace as single mothers. Weidman, White, and Swartz (1988) discovered a wide array of factors—including violence, family criticism, health problems, and financial concerns—that circumscribed poor women's work efforts. Belle's (1982) contextual analysis of the life circumstances of poor women and their families revealed similar barriers to their efforts to escape impoverished conditions.

The voices of the women echo the stresses and difficult life circumstances found in the stories of poor single mothers presented by Valerie Polakow (1993). Similarly, many of the outcomes dovetail with those from Mark Rank's interviews (1994) with fifty welfare families, including single mothers, married couples, single people, and the elderly. These families experience many of the same hardships and work experiences and express similar hopes and dreams as those voiced by the women in this study.

Polakow (1993) and Rank (1994) join with Richard Caputo (1989) and Diana Pearce (1989, 1993), among others, in calling for a broader perspective on the issue of poverty. The outcomes of this research add to the urgency of this call. Through the voices of the women comes the need for a broad-based attack on poverty on a variety of fronts. The past and present circumstances of these women reflect the multiple barriers they encounter. Improving the quality of life for the women and their children requires a broad agenda.

What is needed are national policies that capture this broad perspective. Policy makers need to recognize that only a broad agenda can bring about meaningful improvements in the lives of the women and their children. Such policies and priorities can mobilize and direct the efforts of a variety of institutions—local, state, and federal governments; for-profit and not-for-profit organizations; educational, social, and religious groups; communities and families. The public debate and concomitant actions need to move from the narrow to the broad perspective.

Such a move will not be easy. First of all, we will have to wean ourselves away from a "quick-fix" approach. There are no short-run, simple solutions to complex problems. Developing and implementing a broad plan requires long-term, comprehensive efforts. Asking the wrong questions and hiding our heads behind a narrow focus will not improve the lives and circumstances of the millions of women and children living in poverty. A narrow approach might provide a short-term sense of "doing something," but because it doesn't address the problem, frustrations mount, the problem remains, and new short-term solutions emerge. Nothing really changes, despite the energy expended and rhetoric expounded. Only by working on answers to the broad questions can we, in the long run, bring about a permanent reduction in the number of single women and their children living in poverty.

Second, directly addressing the problem of women and poverty can threaten current institutions and ways of working. For example, the research outcomes reinforce Joan Smith's argument (1984) that the success of the rapidly expanding service sectors is dependent on the low-wage labor of poor women. Lacking education and training, the women rely on these types of jobs for income and as a way to balance their roles as provider and mother. Their low incomes, however, make public assistance a necessary additional support. Upgrading either the working conditions or the women's skills might threaten the viability of some industries. It might even be argued that current welfare expenditures actually subsidize these industries. Confronting such thorny issues is disquieting. But some discomfort may be a small price to pay, compared to the ongoing toll of poverty on the women and their children.

Third, a move toward the broad perspective brings another question to the forefront: Are we willing to facilitate the efforts of single mothers to raise their children well and to obtain an income sufficient to live a decent life? Are we ready to encourage our educational systems, businesses and industries, mental health facilities, and housing and community institutions to be "single-mother friendly"? Three out of every ten U.S. families are headed by a single parent and 86 percent of these single parents are women (U.S. Bureau of the Census 1994, cited in Schmid 1994). Policies and programs that support and encourage the work and child-raising efforts of women raising children alone can mean the difference between poverty and a higher quality of life for these families. Moreover, all working parents benefit from program and institutional flexibility that support their child-raising efforts.

A greater national commitment to helping poor single mothers leave poverty would force us to recognize both the problem and the need for long-term efforts required to eradicate it effectively. As with any change, it will alter the status quo for some and muddy the waters of "the way things should be" for others. Addressing the issues and action recommendations stemming from a broad perspective requires courage and compassion.

Within a broad perspective, consideration of welfare reform issues become only one part of a much larger picture. There is a need for public debates and legislative actions on welfare reform. Proposals to blend work and welfare, improve the enforcement of child-support payments, implement a child-support assurance system or address staffing and bureaucratic inefficiencies in the welfare system (see Spalter-Roth, Hartmann, and Andrews 1992; Garfinkel, Phillips, and Corbett 1992; and Brandwein 1993, among others) speak to shoring up the women's economic base and helping the system better assist its recipients. There is also a need to strengthen our national efforts to eliminate barriers to educational and employment opportunities based on gender or race and to implement national policies providing access to affordable health care and affordable, high-quality child care. For poor single mothers, these become part of a solid foundation upon which to place the stepping stool out of poverty.

The action framework recommendations, rather than just supporting the women, facilitate the women's efforts to support themselves and their families. They are investments in the future. The action framework is not a stop-gap measure, one geared to move women off the edge of poverty into a permanent rut. Rather it is one that offers them hope for fulfilling their basic dreams of a home, a good income, a car that runs, and a future for their children.

The framework for a future points us in this positive direction. Research of this nature can be expanded to include the voices of larger numbers of women. An expanded study would allow for possible demographic differences within the common themes and categories to emerge. Such outcomes would help to fine-tune the action plan and increase its effectiveness. Translating the research outcomes and those from other studies into poverty prevention strategies also needs attention.

Finally, research of this kind needs to be expanded to include the voices of the men. Lillian Rubin (1994), for example, describes the experiences of males and the family circumstances that lead to male violence and betrayal. We need to bring their mates out of the shadows and learn more about their life circumstances. What are the stories behind the disappearing dads and the men troubled by alcohol and drug addiction? What can we learn that can help them? There is much work to be done.

What is needed is leadership and a national commitment to this broad and positive perspective. If national leaders continue to ignore the problem, single mothers will probably stay stuck in the revolving door of moving on and off public assistance. If even that door closes, the outcome for them is bleak. But if policy makers respond, a whole host of programs and activities, many already in place, can be brought together as a coherent, directed effort to improve the quality of the lives of poor single mothers and their children.

Time for a Sea Change

What will fuel the development of national policies that capture the broad perspective, bringing poverty reduction, rather than welfare rolls reduction, to the public forefront? What will activate a broad, comprehensive approach to improving the lives of the women and their children? What will it take to move seriously and with strength on all three fronts of a framework for a future?

The answer lies in listening to the voices of the women. By doing so, we move beyond stereotypes to the women as individuals, with variations in strengths, abilities, and attitudes. Stereotyping, and the distancing it promotes, tends to bring out what people or groups lack in comparison to others. It fosters a deficit model of thinking about impoverished mothers. Looking closely at the women's lives, seeing both uniqueness and commonalities, provides a more comprehensive and positive view of single mothers living in poverty.

The voices of the women reveal their strengths and allow us to embrace their heroic side. We can see them as women of commitment. Neither victim nor scapegoat, they are women overcoming hardships to be mothers and heads of their families. In spite of many difficulties, they struggle to make a life for themselves and their children. Perseverance and willingness to work hard are among their strengths. They are caring and put their children first. These are valuable qualities.

A focus on the framework for a future can be fueled by a transformation of our attitudes and views of poor single mothers. With a sea change in attitudes, we can recognize the women's strengths and provide opportunities that build on their assets, helping the women to forge their own paths out of poverty.

Julie, for instance, and her two young children have been living on roughly $5,000 per year from public assistance. Sometimes she can't afford a pack of gum for the children, but she can always put the sheet on the living room floor and picnic with them. For two years Julie has struggled with balancing the mother-provider roles and handling financial and transportation problems while pursuing further education. Still on public assistance, but armed with new employment skills, she is ready to enter the workforce full-time and begin her slow climb out of poverty.

Julie concluded her story, *"Give us a break. Give us a break. Help us. We are not asking you to give us charity, we are asking for help. Give us the support that we need. Don't treat us like we are menials. We are not, we are humans. We have rights."*

Equipped with a fuller understanding of their lives, we can respond to Julie's plea with actions geared to addressing the needs of mothers in poverty. Such actions can bring about a change in their circumstances. Although the agenda is substantial, it is designed to help the women help themselves. Income opportunities, a social support and linking system, and help and healing will guide the women onto paths that lead out of poverty permanently. The women, because of their position on the margins, have a way to go on this journey. The framework for a future facilitates their efforts to build a life for themselves and their children that is filled with hope and opportunities.

Background Sketches
of the Women

Amelia, thirty-three, has two elementary-school-age children and is divorced. She is white, a high school graduate, and has held an office personnel administrative/supervisory position. Amelia lives in a town and continues to work in clerical positions as they become available.

Anita, twenty-six, has one child in kindergarten. She is white, has never been married, and lives in a town. Anita, a high school graduate, has worked continuously as a waitress and does so now on a part-time basis.

Arlene, thirty-four, has three children, two of elementary school age and one recently graduated from high school. She is divorced, white, and lives in a

NOTE: "Town" refers to a small town, medium-size town, or rural area. "City" refers to a small or large city.

town. A high school graduate, she recently received her associate college degree in business administration. Arlene has just moved off public assistance benefits to start a full-time job as a customer service representative.

Bobbie, thirty-two, has two children, an infant and one of elementary school age. She is white, divorced, and did not complete high school. She lives in a town. Bobbie has held a variety of jobs, primarily factory work and waitressing, and currently works part-time as a bartender.

Carla, twenty-six, has three children, ranging from an infant to elementary school in age. A woman of color, she has never been married, and did not complete high school. She lives in a city. Carla has worked in office maintenance and is currently employed part-time as a telemarketing representative.

Carol, thirty-four, has three children; the oldest is post–high school and the youngest is in elementary school. She is divorced, white, and lives in a city. Carol dropped out of high school, but has since completed her GED and recently completed a two-year dental technician training program. She is actively seeking a job in her degree area.

Connie, twenty-seven, has two children in elementary school and is divorced. She is white, a high school graduate, and has held positions in sales. She lives in a town and works part-time as a hospital clerical. She has definite plans to attend college, working toward an associate or bachelor's degree in nursing.

Emily, thirty-three, has four young children, ranging from an infant to elementary school in age. She is divorced, white, and lives in a town. Emily graduated from high school and completed two years of college. She worked briefly as an art instructor, but now cares for her children full-time.

Eva, twenty-two, has two children, a preschooler and one in elementary school. A woman of color, she has never married, and did not graduate from high school. She lives in a city. Eva has held a variety of jobs, including auto transporter. She would like to be a policewoman.

Faith, thirty-two, has two teen-age children. She has never married. A woman of color, she lives in a city. Faith graduated from high school and works part time as a dietary aide in a hospital.

Gloria, forty-two, has five children, all teenagers or young adults. A white woman, she is divorced and lives in a town. Gloria dropped out of high school. She has since completed her GED and recently received an associate degree from a business college. She is actively seeking full-time employment.

Irene, thirty-three, has one child in elementary school. She has never married and lives in a city. A woman of color, she is a high school graduate. Irene has some vocational training in hotel work, and would like to study management in a community college.

Jean, thirty-two, has five children, ranging from a kindergartener to a young teenager. She is white, separated, and lives in a town. Jean dropped out of high school, but has since completed her GED. She works in a food-processing plant but is looking for a full-time clerical position.

Jessie, thirty-nine, has four children, two young adults and two in elementary school. She is white, divorced, and lives in a town. She did not complete high school but has since received her GED. Jessie has worked mainly as a waitress and hostess in restaurants and for a short time had a home-based furniture restoring business.

Joy, twenty-four, has two preschool children. A woman of color, she has never married and did not complete high school. She lives in a city and has worked in telecommunications. Joy is taking preparatory courses for a medical assistant study program.

Judy, twenty-nine, has two children, an infant and one of elementary school age. A white woman, she has never married and did not complete high school. She lives in a town. Judy has always worked as a waitress and is returning shortly to that job.

Julie, thirty-five, has two children in elementary school. She is white, divorced, and a high school graduate. She lives in a town. Julie recently received her associate college degree in computer applications and computerized office accounting. She is actively seeking a position in her field.

LaVerne, thirty-four, has one child in elementary school. She is white, has never married, and is a high school graduate. She lives in a town. LaVerne has held a variety of jobs, primarily in factories, and currently works part-time as a barber.

Leona, forty, has five children, two young adults, two teenagers, and one of elementary school age. She never married and dropped out of high school. Leona, a woman of color, lives in a city. She has held few jobs, and is enrolled in a preparatory skills class.

Marie, thirty-one, has three children in elementary school. She is white, separated, and a high school graduate. She lives in a town. Marie has worked in a civil service clerical position for seven years.

Marilyn, thirty-two, has three children, two teenagers and one of elementary school age. She is white, divorced, and lives in a town. She did not complete high school. Marilyn has held a variety of jobs, primarily factory and waitressing work. Her youngest child has medical problems.

Meg, twenty-one, has an infant. She is white, has never been married, and is a high school graduate. She lives in a town. Meg works part-time as a waitress.

Nancy, twenty-five, has three elementary-school-age children. She is white, has never married, and is a high school graduate. She lives in a town. Nancy works part-time as an occupational therapy aide and is in school part-time, studying for an associate degree in the same field.

Pat, twenty-seven, has four children; the youngest is an infant and the oldest is in elementary school. She is white, divorced, and lives in a town. She dropped out of high school but has since completed her GED. She recently received an associate college degree. Pat is employed full-time as a paralegal.

Renata, thirty-seven, has two teenage children. A woman of color, she has never married and did not complete high school. She lives in a city. Renata has held a variety of factory jobs and had to leave her last one due to medical problems.

Sally, thirty-seven, has two teenage children. A white woman, she is divorced and a high school graduate. She lives in a town. Sally has held a variety of jobs, primarily waitressing and factory work. She has medical problems.

Sheila, forty, has three children: a young adult, a teenager, and a preschooler. A woman of color, she is separated and a high school graduate. She lives in a city. Sheila has held waitressing and secretarial jobs. She is applying for jobs in maintenance and administration.

Susan, twenty-two, has one child in kindergarten. A white woman, she is divorced and lives in a town. She did not complete high school, but has since received her GED. Susan recently received her certificate as a nurse's aide and is working part-time in that position.

Ursula, forty, has three children, two young adults and a teenager. She is a woman of color, is separated, and is a high school graduate. She lives in a city.

Her youngest child has had lifelong medical problems. Ursula has volunteered as a school sports coach and is in preparatory courses for study as a medical lab technician.

Vicki, thirty, has two elementary-school-age children. She is white, divorced, and a high school graduate. She lives in a town. She has held a variety of factory jobs, and until recently was employed in nursing home maintenance and caregiving. Vicki has medical problems and is seeking factory work.

APPENDIX. Sample Selection, Interview Design, Interview Process, and Procedures

How Were the Women Selected?

The study was done with the cooperation and assistance of five county assistance agencies in a large eastern state. Each office provided the names of women who were single heads of households, receiving some form of public assistance, raising one or more children eighteen years or younger, and who were working or had some work experience. A representative in each office first contacted the women, described the study in brief, assured them of confidentiality, and asked if they would be willing to participate on a volunteer basis. The researcher was identified as a professor and not affiliated with any county assistance agency. No name was forwarded without the prior consent of the woman. The agencies were selected on the basis of their rural versus urban county populations, with an attempt to yield a two-thirds rural and one-third urban group composition. There was no mention of or request for any particular racial mix in any of the counties.

Interviews were arranged with each of the thirty women. Each interview lasted from sixty to ninety minutes. The women engaged actively in the interview process and several wanted to continue discussions beyond the time allotted. Handwritten thank-you notes were sent to each of the thirty women who participated in the study.

What Did I Ask Them?

The interview was designed to cover basic demographics, work experiences, and past and present life circumstances. The questions were semistructured and open ended. Basic demographics included questions about age, marital history, number of children, education, and duration and type of county assistance received. The work experiences questions sought to get a reasonably in-depth look at their past and present work experiences. The women were asked to describe, in detail, one or more jobs, including the work itself, supervision, and co-workers. Questions about how they obtained the job, forms of training, and performance evaluations were asked about jobs held. Open-ended questions included: Describe a time on the job when you felt really good/happy (or bad/not happy). What is your dream job and how will you get there? What does work/working mean to you? If a woman was finishing some form of job or educational training, various aspects of the training were discussed.

Past and present life circumstances were probed under a variety of topic headings. These headings included: early years, helpers and inhibitors, personal relationships, children, finances, and the future. Some specific questions were: Tell me about your growing up years. What (or who) makes your life easier? harder? Tell me about your friends. What are the joys and difficulties of raising children alone? Tell me how you manage your money. What do you wish for yourself?

The analyses and presentation of the information, such as income and expenditures, are based entirely on the self-reports of the women.

The Interview Process

Prior to the start of each interview, the following description was presented to the woman:

This is a study of women, work and the problems of raising children alone. You have my assurances of confidentiality. I do not work for any assistance office and nothing that you tell me will be told to your assistance office. I do, however, need your information and in some cases your exact words. I can assure you of anonymity. I will never use your name and will disguise various specifics about you. If there are any questions that you don't want to answer, feel free to say so. Please don't tell me anything about yourself you are not comfortable with. I am only interested in the experiences that you want to share with me.

I will write up the results in either a book or several articles, or both. I hope to use the results to influence policy makers to understand the issues of single mothers and work.

Do I have your permission to do this interview? I need to tape the interview. Do I have your permission to do so?

The demographics were asked first, followed by the work-experience questions. The work-experience questions were asked before the life circumstances questions to give the woman time to get comfortable in the situation.

The semistructured and open-ended questions formed the core of the interview and during the course of each interview all or most of these questions were eventually asked. In most cases, however, the woman's "story" usually took over the interview process and the interview moved at its own pace and in its own way.

As the interviewing progressed, a pattern of revealing a "surprise circumstance" emerged. No life history was what it seemed at the beginning of the interview. The surprises ranged from physical abuse by the husband to a prison term to a negative childhood event. These "surprises" were usually transforming events in the woman's life.

It became clear during the course of the interviewing that withholding judgment and demonstrating understanding was an important part of this interviewing process. Many of the incidents and histories, such as sexual abuse, physical violence, and criminal acts, were emotionally laden. It was important to accept the information and be supportive of the woman's reactions to these events in a neutral but concerned manner.

Interviews were conducted in the homes of twenty-two of the thirty women: twenty rural/town women and two urban women. Eight other interviews, with urban women, were conducted in a private conference room at the assistance office. Children were present for all or part of fourteen of the interviews. In two cases, the interviewee's mother and one or more family members were also present or nearby.

As part of the home interview procedure, impressions of the homes, such as room sizes and available space, as well as the setting—that is, trailer park, apartment complex, rural area—were recorded. Drawings were also made of the physical layout of each residence. For all the interviews, notations were made as to the characteristics of the rural area, town, or city in which the women lived. All names used, including those of the women, the people to whom they refer, any local or state programs, and areas, towns, and cities are pseudonyms.

References

Abramovitz, Mimi. 1988. *Regulating the lives of women: Social welfare policy from Colonial times to present*. Boston: South End Press.

American Association of University Women. 1992. How schools shortchange girls. Executive Summary. Washington, D.C.: American Association of University Women Foundation.

Amott, Theresa. 1993. A wage of one's own. *Church and Society*, March/April, 12–23.

Amott, Theresa, and Julie Matthaei. 1991. *Race, gender, and work: A multicultural economic history of women in the United States*. Boston: South End Press.

Bane, Mary Jo, and David Ellwood, 1994. *Welfare realities: From rhetoric to reform*. Cambridge, Mass.: Harvard University Press.

Belle, Deborah, ed. 1982. *Lives in stress: Women and depression*. Beverly Hills, Calif.: Sage.

Blumer, Herbert. 1970. Methodological principles of empirical science. In *Sociological methods: A sourcebook*, Norman K. Denzim, ed., pp. 20–39. Chicago: Aldine.

Bogdan, Robert, and Steven J. Taylor. 1975. *Introduction to qualitative research methods: A phenomenological approach to the social sciences.* New York: John Wiley.

Brandwein, Ruth A. 1993. Women's reality: Making work pay and making welfare work. Paper presented at the conference "Women and Welfare Reform: Women's Poverty, Women's Opportunities, and Women's Welfare," sponsored by the Institute for Women's Policy Research, Washington, D.C., October.

Bray, Rosemary L. 1994. Remember the children. *Ms.*, September/October, 38–41.

Caputo, Richard K. 1989. Limits of welfare reform. *Social Casework: The Journal of Contemporary Social Work* 70 (7): 85–95.

Carstens, Catherine M. 1991. The new technology of poverty lending. *Business Mexico* 1 (8): 28–31, 51.

Coleman, Elizabeth. 1993. Breaking out of the pink-collar ghetto. *Ford Foundation Report*. Spring: 24–27.

Cooper, Mary A. 1993. Beyond stereotypes: Women as heads of households. *Church and Society*, March/April, 24–36.

Corcoran, Mary, Greg J. Duncan, and Martha S. Hill. 1984. The economic fortunes of women and children: Lessons from the panel study of income dynamics. *Signs* 10 (2): 232–48.

Cowell, Susan. 1993. Family policy: A union approach. In *Women and unions: Forging a partnership*. Dorothy Sue Cobble, ed., pp. 115–28. Ithaca, N.Y.: ILR Press.

Davidson, Chandler, and Charles Gaitz. 1974. "Are the poor different?" A comparison of work behavior and attitudes among the urban poor and nonpoor. *Social Problems* 22 (2): 229–45.

DeParle, Jason. 1992. A law meant to shift people on welfare to job pays off. *New York Times*, April 23.

Dudenhefer, Paul. 1993. Poverty in the rural United States. *Focus* 15 (1): 37–46.

Ellwood, David T. 1988. *Poor support: Poverty in the American family*. New York: Basic Books.

Friedlander, Frank, and Stuart Greenberg. 1971. Effect of job attitudes, training, and organizational climate on performance of the hardcore unemployed. *Journal of Applied Psychology* 55: 287–95.

Friedman, Thomas L. 1994. Foreign-aid agency shifts to problems back home. *New York Times*, June 26.

Gardner, S., C. Dean, and D. McKaig. 1989. Responding to differences in the classroom: The politics of knowledge, class, and sexuality. *Sociology of Education* 62: 64–74.

Garfinkel, Irwin, and Sara McLanahan. 1986. *Single mothers and their children: A new American dilemma*. Washington, D.C.: Urban Institute Press.

Garfinkel, Irwin, Elizabeth Phillips, and Tom Corbett. 1992. A new way to fight child poverty and welfare dependence: A child support assurance system (CSAS). Working paper, National Center for Children in Poverty, Columbia University School of Public Health.

Garvin, Charles D., Audrey D. Smith, and William J. Reid, eds. 1978. *The work incentive experience*. Montclair, N.J.: Allanheld, Osmun & Co.

Glaser, Barney G., and Anselm L. Strauss. 1967. *The discovery of grounded theory: Strategies for qualitative research*. Chicago: Aldine.

Goodwin, Leonard. 1972. *Do the poor want to work? A social-psychological study of work orientations*. Washington, D.C.: Brookings Institution.

Gould, Sara K., Deborah Stern, and Jing Lyman. 1989. Supporting women's self-employment: A new training option. In *Job training for women: The promise and limits of public policy*, Sharon L. Harlan and Ronnie J. Steinberg, eds., pp. 224–46. Philadelphia: Temple University Press.

Greenberg, Mark. 1992. Welfare reform on a budget: What's happening in JOBS. Washington, D.C.: Center for Law and Social Policy.

Gueron, Judith M., and Edward Pauly. 1991. *From welfare to work*. New York: Russell Sage Foundation.

Hanson, Russell L., and John T. Hartman. 1994. Do welfare magnets attract? Discussion Paper No. 1028-94, Institute for Research on Poverty (IRP).

Harlan, Sharon L., and Ronnie J. Steinberg, eds. 1989. *Job training for women: The promise and limits of public policy*. Philadelphia: Temple University Press.

Harris, Kathleen M. 1993. Work and welfare among single mothers in poverty. *American Journal of Sociology* 99 (2): 317–52.

Haveman, Robert H., and John Karl Scholz. 1994. The Clinton welfare plan: Will it end poverty as we know it? Discussion Paper No. 1037-94, Institute for Research on Poverty (IRP).

Henderson, Cathy, and Cecilia Ottinger. 1985. College degree . . . still a ladder to success? *Journal of College Placement* (Spring): 35–38.

Irwin, John. 1987. Reflections on ethnography. *Journal of Contemporary Ethnography* 16 (1): 41–48.

Jaffe, Peter G., David A. Wolfe, and Sarah K. Wilson. 1990. *Children of battered women*. Newbury Park, Calif.: Sage.

Kahn, Arnold, and Janice D. Yoder. 1989. The psychology of women and conservatism: Rediscovering social change. *Psychology of Women Quarterly* 13: 417–32.

Kissman, Kris. 1990. Women in blue-collar occupations: An exploration in constraints and facilitators. *Journal of Sociology and Social Welfare* 17 (3): 139–49.

Knive-Ingraham, Kathleen D. 1985. The impact of a brief, intensive group counselling program on single mothers' perceptions of family functioning. *International Journal of Women's Studies* 8 (4): 319–27.

Koss, Mary, Lisa Goodman, Louise Fitzgerald, Nancy Russo, and Gwendolyn Keita, eds. 1994. *No safe haven: Male violence against women at home, at work, and in the community*. Washington, D.C.: American Psychological Association.

Latack, Janina, Bonnie Roach, Sasen Josephs, and Mitchell Levine. 1987. Carpenter apprentices: Comparison of career transitions for men and women. *Journal of Applied Psychology* 72 (3): 393–400.

MacKenzie, Dale A. 1985. Wife abuse: An overview of salient issues. *Canadian Journal of Community Mental Health* 4 (1): 65–79.

Marshall, Nancy. 1982. The public welfare system: Regulation and dehumanization. In *Lives in stress: Women and depression*. Deborah Belle, ed., pp. 96–108. Beverly Hills: Sage.

Martin, Douglas. 1994. Hiring welfare recipients and making them management. *New York Times*, May 21.

McGrath, Ellen, Gwendolyn Keita, Bonnie Strickland, and Nancy Russo, eds. 1990. *Women and depression: Risk factors and treatment issues*. Washington, D.C.: American Psychological Association.

Messer, Stanley, and Paul Lehrer. 1976. Short-term groups with female welfare clients in a job-training program. *Professional Psychology* (August): 352–58.

Miller, Dorothy C. 1990. *Women and social welfare: A feminist analysis*. New York: Praeger.

Morrison, Wendy, Gwen Page, Mary Sehl, and Heather Smither. 1986. Single mothers in Canada: An analysis. *Canadian Journal of Community Mental Health* 5 (2): 37–47.

Mulroy, Elizabeth, and Marcy Pitt-Catsouphes. 1994. Single parents in the workplace. Policy paper, Boston University Center on Work and Family. Boston, Mass.

Mulvey, A. 1988. Community psychology and feminism: Lessons and commonalities. *Journal of Community Psychology* 16: 70–84.

Nelton, S. 1989. The age of the woman entrepreneur. *Nation's Business*, May, 22–26.

New York Times. 1988. A single-parent home that sponsors dreams. May 19.

O'Farrell, Brigid, and Suzanne Moore. 1993. Unions, hard hats, and women workers. In *Women and unions: Forging a partnership*, Dorothy Sue Cobble, ed., pp. 69–84. Ithaca, N.Y.: ILR Press.

O'Leary, Virginia. 1972. The Hawthorne effect in reverse: Trainee orientation for the hard-core unemployed woman. *Journal of Applied Psychology* 56 (6): 491–94.

Pavetti, LaDonna A. 1993. The dynamics of welfare and work: Exploring the process by which women work their way off of welfare. Malcolm Wiener Center for Social Policy Working Papers: Dissertation Series, John F. Kennedy School of Government, Harvard University. Cambridge, Mass.

Pearce, Diana M. 1978. The feminization of poverty: Women, work, and welfare. *Urban and Social Change Review* 11: 28–36.

———. 1989. The feminization of poverty: A second look. Paper presented at the Annual Meeting of the American Sociological Association, San Francisco, August.

———. 1993. Filling the half-full glass: Designing a welfare system that works for women. Paper presented at the conference "Women and Welfare Reform: Women's Poverty, Women's Opportunities, and Women's Welfare," sponsored by the Institute for Women's Policy Research, Washington, D.C., October.

Pendleton, Scott. 1990. Chicago program helps women on welfare return to work. *Christian Science Monitor*, December 13.

Polakow, Valerie. 1993. *Lives on the edge: Single mothers and their children in the other America.* Chicago: University of Chicago Press.

Porter, Kathryn, H. 1989. *Poverty in rural America: A national overview.* Washington, D.C.: Center on Budget and Policy Priorities.

Rabin, Jack, and Kevin E. Moore. 1991. Pennsylvania welfare reform demonstration project: Final report. Executive Summary, Institute of State and Regional Affairs, Penn State Harrisburg, Middletown, Pa.

Rank, Mark R. 1994. *Living on the edge: The realities of welfare in America.* New York: Columbia University Press.

Reid, Pamela M. 1993. Poor women in psychological research. *Psychology of Women Quarterly* 17 (2): 133–50.

Resnick, Gary. 1985. The short- and long-term impact of a competency-based program for disadvantaged women. *Journal of Social Service Research* 7 (4): 37–49.

Riger, Stephanie. 1992. Epistemological debates, feminist voices. *American Psychologist* 47 (6): 730–40.

Robins, Philip K., and Paul Fronstin. 1993. Welfare benefits and family-size decisions of never-married women. Discussion Paper No. 1022-93, Institute for Research on Poverty (IRP).

Rubin, Lillian B. 1994. *Families on the fault line: America's working class speaks about the family, the economy, race and ethnicity.* New York: HarperCollins.

Schiller, Bradley R. 1973. Empirical studies of welfare dependency: A survey. *Journal of Human Resources* 8 (supplement): 19–32.

Schmid, Randolf E. 1994. The American family is no longer Ward, June, Wally, and the Beav. *Gettysburg Times*, August 10.

Shapiro, Isaac. 1992. *White poverty in America.* Washington, D.C.: Center on Budget and Policy Priorities.

Sidel, Ruth. 1986. *Women and children last: The plight of poor women in affluent America.* New York: Penguin Books.

Smith, Joan. 1984. The paradox of women's poverty: Wage earning women and economic transformation. *Signs* 10 (24): 291–310.

Spalter-Roth, Roberta M., Heidi Hartmann, and Linda M. Andrews. 1990. "Mothers, children, and low-wage work: The ability to earn a family wage." Paper presented at the 85th meeting of the American Sociological Association, August.

———. 1992. *Combining work and welfare.* Washington, D.C.: Institute for Women's Policy Research.

Spalter-Roth, Roberta, Enrique Soto, and Lily Zandniapour. 1994. Micro-enterprise and women: The viability of self-employment as a strategy for alleviating poverty. Washington, D.C.: Institute for Women's Policy Research (from Research in Brief, July 1994).

Tableman, Betty, Deborah Marciniak, Diane Johnson, and Roberta Rodgers. 1982. Stress management training for women on public assistance. *American Journal of Community Psychology* 10 (3): 357–67.

Tienda, Marta, and Haya Stier. 1991. Joblessness and shiftlessness: Labor force activity in Chicago's inner city. In *The urban underclass,* Christopher Jencks and Paul Peterson, eds., pp. 135-54. Washington, D.C.: Brookings Institution.

U.S. Bureau of the Census. 1992. *Poverty in the United States: 1991.* Current Population Reports, Series P-60, No. 181. Washington, D.C.: U.S. Government Printing Office.

———. 1993. *Poverty in the United States: 1992.* Current Population Reports, Series P-60, No. 185. Washington, D.C.: U.S. Government Printing Office.

U.S. General Accounting Office. 1991. *Mother-only families: Low earnings will keep many children in poverty.* April. GAO/HRD, 91–62.

Walker, Lenore E. A. 1984. *The battered woman syndrome.* New York: Springer.

Walshok, Mary L. 1981. *Blue collar women: Pioneers on the male frontier.* Garden City, N.Y.: Anchor Press.

Weidman, John, Richard White, and B. Katherine Swartz. 1988. Training women on welfare for "high-tech" jobs. *Evaluation and Program Planning* 11: 105–14.

Whittington, Barbara. 1986. Life skills for single-parent women: A program note. *Canadian Journal of Community Mental Health* 5 (2): 103–9.

Wider Opportunities for Women, Inc. 1993. *Accomplishments of the Nontraditional Employment Training (NET) Project at one and one-half years.* Washington, D.C.

Wilkerson, Isabel. 1994. Taste of middle class for welfare mothers. *New York Times,* February 10.

Williams, Angela C. 1994. Reclaiming the "Welfare Queen." *Equal Means* 2 (2): 27–28.

Wirt, J., L. Murasicin, D. Goodwin, and R. Meyer. 1989. National assessment of vocational education: Summary of findings and recommendations. Washington, D.C.: U.S. Dept. of Education.

"Women and Poverty." 1984. *Signs* 10 (2): special issue.

Worell, Judith. 1988. Single mothers: From problems to policies. *Women and Therapy* 7 (4): 3–13.

Zill, Nicholas, Kristin A. Moore, Christine W. Nord, and Thumar Stief. 1991. "Welfare mothers as potential employees: A statistical profile based on national survey data." Washington, D.C.: Child Trends, Inc.

Index

earned-income tax credit (EITC), 86
economic independence, 126; barriers to,
    10–13
education, 8, 39; absence of, 27, 28; assis-
    tance, 97; lack of, 78, 105; limited, 36; post-
    secondary, 126; returning for, 50–53, 62
EITC (earned-income tax credit), 86
elderly care, 129
electronics jobs, 127
employee ownership, 133
employment: counseling, 135; leaving welfare
    for, 9; security, 77
encouragement: absence of, 94; lack of, 92;
    on the job, 79–80
enforcement system: child support, 110, 112,
    154
entrepreneurship, 131–33, 135
evictions, 33

factories, 30; piece-rate workers, 86; work in,
    69, 70–74; 77, 78, 80, 82, 87
families: balancing work and, 76– 77, 91, 97;
    commitment to, 36; criticism by, 152;
    headed by women, 15; help for battered,
    145; nonsupportive, 11, 27, 39, 91, 92,
    101–103; single mothers and, 8; supportive,
    101
Family Support Act (1988), 7, 97
fathers: absent, 62–68
federal poverty threshold (1992), 86
female-headed families: with children, 5, 16;
    in rural areas, 15
female occupations, 127, 129
feminization of poverty, 4
file clerks, 19, 46, 81
flexibility: for child-care providers, 144; job,
    69, 74, 76–78, 82
food-processing plant employees, 19
food stamps, 18, 20, 45, 47, 56, 57, 97, 106,
    109, 110
Foundation for International Community As-
    sistance, 132
framework for action, 154; components of,
    123–24, 138; foundation for, 151
friends: support from, 91–92, 101–102
fuel assistance, 56, 99
full-time employment, 56; easing transition to,
    139; and poverty line, 5

GED, 57, 70, 98, 126; alternatives to, 50; at-
    tending school for, 42, 52, 101, 104, 147
gender: barriers based on, 154; and discrimi-
    nation, 126, 134, 141; and poverty, 9
Glaser, Barney, 21
glass ceiling, 142
Goodwin, Leonard, 12, 15
grounded-theory perspective, 21
Gueron, Judith, 7

Hanson, Russell, 6
hard-core unemployed (HCU), 11
Hartman, John, 6
Head Start, 48
healing. *See* help and healing
health care, 9; affordable, 139; fields of, 129
health problems, 11, 13, 152; and job loss, 83;
    job-threatening, 84
heat assistance, 56, 99
help and healing, 124, 138, 144–49, 151, 156;
    for domestic violence, 145–46, 148
Henderson, Cathy, 126
high school: degree, 126; dropouts, 29, 30,
    126; graduation, 30
high wages: in blue-collar trades, 128
hiring: bias in, 133
holidays: and lack of money, 60, 62
home health care industry: career promotion
    in, 133
home interview procedure, 166
homeless shelters, 114–15
homeless women, 140
homes: women in their, 23–26, 166
hotel and restaurant management, 129
housing, 9, 21, 22; and bureaucracies, 114–15;
    help with, 47, 101; need for affordable, 140;
    neighborhood, 112; and renovation skills,
    128; and Section 8, 45, 113; subsidized, 56,
    113; transitional, 146, 147; waiting lists for,
    113
HUD (Department of Housing and Urban De-
    velopment), 113

imprisonment, 33, 66, 111, 165; of abusive fa-
    thers, 31–32, 52; for drug possession, 33;
    and job applications, 39
income opportunities, 151, 156; and college
    degree, 126; defined, 123–24; discussed,

About the Author

Virginia E. Schein, an organizational psychologist, is professor and chair of the Management Department at Gettysburg College. She received her undergraduate degree from Cornell University and her Ph.D. in industrial psychology from New York University. She has taught at the Wharton School and the City University of New York, and she has served as head of personnel research at Metropolitan Life Insurance Company.

A pioneer in the field of women in management, Schein is recognized internationally for her groundbreaking research on sex-role stereotypes and requisite management characteristics. She is also widely known for her work on the issues of enhancing women's opportunities in the workplace, on power and politics in organizations, and on organizational change.

She is a past president of the Metropolitan New York Association for Applied Psychology, and she has been active in the Division of Industrial and Organizational Psychology of the American Psychological Association and in the Women in Management Division of the Academy of Management.